Detail from a Neal Storage Company
1925 map of Cleveland and suburbs.
Richard F. Hershey Collection

All Luna Park newspaper ads that appear throughout this book, unless otherwise noted, are from the Cleveland *Plain Dealer*, 1905-1929.

LUNA PARK

CLEVELAND'S FAIRYLAND OF PLEASURE

David W. Francis and Diane DeMali Francis

Entrance to Luna Park, Cleveland, O.

CLEVELAND'S FAIRYLAND OF PLEASURE

David W. Francis and
Diane DeMali Francis

Amusement Park Books, Inc.
Fairview Park, Ohio

**Also by David W. Francis
and Diane DeMali Francis**

Summit Beach Park: Akron's Coney Island
Cedar Point: The Queen of American Watering Places

Other titles by Amusement Park Books, Inc.

Euclid Beach Park is Closed for the Season
Euclid Beach Park - A Second Look
Harry G. Traver: Legends of Terror
The Incredible Scream Machine: A History of the Roller Coaster
Conneaut Lake Park: the First 100 Years of Fun
Cedar Point: The Queen of American Watering Places

DEDICATION

To the City of Cleveland,
whose colorful past, vital present, and
promising future makes its two hundredth year
a celebration of the
"Best Location in the Nation."

Published by

Amusement Park Books, Inc.

20925 Mastick Road
Fairview Park, Ohio 44126
(216) 331-6429

03 02 01 00 99 98 97 96   7 6 5 4 3 2 1

ISBN 0-935408-05-3
Library of Congress Number 95-83957

– Book Designed by Edward Chukayne –

TABLE OF CONTENTS

FOREWORD

For those familiar with the city of Cleveland's past, reminiscences often lead to musings about a *different time*, eventually bringing to light Euclid Beach Park as a subject of nostalgia. For some, that place may be the only amusement park associated with Ohio's largest metropolitan area. But, a few remember, and others have heard of, Cleveland's *other* park, that rivaled the numerous outdoor amusement facilities that were present in the area from 1900 through the 1930s.

Luna Park opened on Cleveland's east side in 1905. It was located where Woodland Avenue and Woodhill Road meet, near what is now East 110th Street, just south of the Baldwin Reservoir. Very different from Euclid Beach, Luna Park was patterned after the Coney Island, New York, phenomena of the same name that opened in 1903. With thousands of electric lights, the vision of Luna was of lavish illumination and a merry mixture of eclectic architecture. The people of Cleveland were dazzled, responding with a sense of awe as a result of the spectacle that was Luna Park. It was an immediate hit!

Luna Park thrived in its early days, survived the tumult of World War One, entered the time of flap-

pers, speakeasies and jazz and was crippled by Prohibition. Some of its attractions ranged from the somewhat demure Shoot-the-Chutes, the Scenic Railway and carousel to the spectacles of dirigible flights, racy girlie shows and exotic dancers. Luna Park flourished, faltered and then quickly faded, failing to open in 1930.

However, during the twenty-five seasons of operation, Luna Park was not just Cleveland's *other* park, but often was the city's most popular summer spot. The story of *Cleveland's Fairyland of Pleasure*, a slogan often used in the second decade of the century, is told in a fascinating manner by David W. and Diane DeMali Francis. The details of the times, mood and people associated with Cleveland's *other* park are graphically captured by means of careful research, generous illustration and good humor.

Amusement Park Books is pleased and proud to be the publishers chosen by the Francis' to bring this overlooked part of Cleveland's history to print as the city celebrates its 200th year.

Amusement Park Books, Inc.   Lee O. Bush
                                Richard F. Hershey

ACKNOWLEDGEMENTS

As a child growing up during the 1950s and 1960s, I was one of thousands of Cleveland-area youngsters who thought that Euclid Beach Park was the greatest place on earth. Cedar Point had not yet started its renaissance, and all of the other area parks were paled in comparison to The Beach. My love of Euclid Beach was enhanced by stories my grandmother told about the park's early days. Born in 1889, she remembered clearly the days before the Thriller, the Flying Turns, and even the Racing Coaster. At one point I suggested that Euclid Beach must have been a wonderful place in the "old days." She answered that indeed it was, but it couldn't match Luna Park. She recalled Luna's opening in 1905 and told dozens of stories about a park that sounded more mythical than real.

By the 1970s, my interest in the history of amusement parks and summer resorts led me to begin researching the park industry. Soon, I learned that my family had a number of connections to Luna Park. My mother's aunt owned a bungalow just one street from the park. On summer nights, the upstairs porch offered a grand view of Luna's lights. Needless to say, my mother and her family made many visits to the park. On my father's side of the family, I learned that an uncle, Albert Chatfield, operated the photo studio that was located next to Luna's Shoot-the-Chutes.

These family ties, along with the wonderful stories that my grandmother told about Luna, enticed me to begin researching the park's background. Eventually, my research resulted in a short article, but plans for a full-scale book about Luna were shelved while my wife and I completed books about Cedar Point and Summit Beach Park.

After years of research and interviews with numerous people, the historical picture of Cleveland's Luna Park began to emerge. It was, in fact, more amazing and colorful than my grandmother's recollections had led me to believe.

During the course of my research, scores of people and institutions assisted in uncovering information and photos. Without their help, this book would not have been possible.

The assistance of amusement park historian Charles J. Jacques, Jr. was indispensable. He graciously shared many documents and photos from his personal collection at a time when he was busy with his own writing projects. The late Fred Fried, despite being deeply involved in preparing a history of Coney Island, took the time to locate photos of Luna Park's carousel and of Fred Ingersoll.

I owe a debt of thanks to the staff of the Wadsworth Public Library, and especially to Bobbie Richards who endured almost endless requests for the interlibrary loan of newspapers and other materials.

Among the many people who assisted with information, photographs, or memories of Luna Park were: James Abbate, president of the National Amusement Park Historical Association; Mr. and Mrs. Boyd Berry; Paul Bierley; M. Frederick Bramley; Phil Bramley; Michael Branch; Betty Brawley; Norman Buckholtz; Joe Cali; Russell Croucher; Frances Davenport; Connie Doan, Charlotte Girsch; Sophie Goodman; Gary Grant; Ward Grant; Catherine Gugliotta; Dominic A. Gugliotta; Dorothy Gugliotta; David Hall; Marilyn Halstead; Susie Hanson; Jack Hiddlestone; Bob Hope;

Frank M. Hruby; Paul S. Korol; Ted Krause; Christine L. Krosel; Beulah Larsen; Gertrude B. Lint; Eleanor D. Loede; Sam Marshall; Dale F. Menger; Ellen S. Milne; Katherine J. McCarrick; Jan McKay; Dorothy Noga; Barry F. S. Norman; Dick Peery; Dr. F. F. Peterka; Kathleen Pownall; Robert Preedy; Constance Rehak; Susan Remchick; Tina Russell; Loras Schissel; Ann K. Sindelar; Gilbert L. Smith, Jr.; Terry Stahurski; Ed Thyret, Sr.; Bill Tomko; Jean Tussey; Charles Wood; Mary Clare Yarham; and Bruce Young.

The museums, libraries, organizations, and companies that provided invaluable assistance include: Atlantic City Free Public Library; Ardmore (Oklahoma) Public Library; Arlington County Public Library, Virginia; Buffalo and Erie County Historical Society; Case Western Reserve University; Chicago Historical Society; Circus World Museum; Cleveland Metroparks Zoo; Cleveland Museum of Natural History; Cleveland *Plain Dealer*; Cleveland *Press* Collection, Cleveland State University; Cleveland Public Library; Cleveland Trinidad Paving Company; Colorado Historical Society; Connecticut Historical Society; Cornell University; Curt Teich Postcard Archives; Danville (Virginia) Historical Society; Detroit Public Library; DeWitt Historical Society (Ithaca, New York); Diocese of Cleveland Archives; City of Euclid; Free Library of Philadelphia; Hartford Public Library; Hawaiian Historical Society; Heritage Society (Houston, Texas); Historical Society of Seattle and King County; Historical Society of Washington, D.C.; Hope Enterprises, Inc.; Indiana Historical Society; Indiana University; John Carroll University; Lackawanna Historical Society (Scranton, Pennsylvania);

Lake County Historical Society; Library of Congress; Los Angeles Public Library; Maryland Historical Society; Medina Public Library; Miami-Dade Public Library; Millville (New Jersey) Public Library; Motorcycle Heritage Museum; Museum of History and Industry (Seattle, Washington); National Archives; National Association of Letter Carriers, Branch 40; Ohio Army National Guard, Adjutant General's Department; Ohio Historical Society; State of Ohio, Secretary of State; Schenectady County Historical Society; Seattle Public Library; Six Flags Over Mid-America; Smithsonian Institution; United States Army Historical Institute; United States Military Academy; Vestal Press, Limited; Virginia-North Carolina Piedmont Genealogical Society; West Virginia Division of Culture and History; and Western Reserve Historical Society.

A debt of gratitude is owed to Ginger Toth. Over a period of several years she fielded numerous telephone calls about Luna Park, handled a large volume of correspondence and helped prepare the final draft for publication.

Finally, I owe my greatest debt to my wife Diane, who co-authored our books on Cedar Point and Summit Beach. Diane assisted with research, helped gather photographs, and endured endless conversations about Luna Park. When this book was near completion, she took time from her own busy schedule to edit the manuscript.

Wadsworth, Ohio   February 11, 1995

The entrance to Coney Island's Luna Park provided a sampling of the architectural wonderland that awaited visitors beyond the admission gates.
Cleveland Public Library

 HAPTER ONE

THE ORIGINS OF LUNA PARK

CONEY ISLAND, NEW YORK

During the first ten years of the twentieth century, New York's Coney Island was the undisputed capital of the world's amusement park industry. Innovations that were successful at Coney Island were quickly imitated and duplicated elsewhere. Rides, shows, games, and novelty foods that were born at Coney were reproduced by showmen throughout the world. Among Coney's most enduring inventions were the hot dog, first served by Charles Feltman during the 1870s, and the roller coaster, premiered by LaMarcus A. Thompson in 1884. Even when considering all of the island's contributions to the amusement industry, perhaps Coney's greatest export was the name, the format, and the mystique of Luna Park.

By 1905, Coney Island was the home of three of the country's largest and finest amusement parks: Steeplechase Park (1897-1964), Dreamland Park (1904-1911), and Luna Park (1903-1946). Although Steeplechase enjoyed the longest life, it was Luna Park that became a household name in pre-1920 America. In addition, Luna Park was known on every continent and its name was translated into more than a dozen languages.

Coney's Luna Park was the child of two brilliant showmen, Elmer "Skip" Dundy (1862-1907) and Frederic Thompson (1873-1919). Dundy was a financial wizard and Thompson was a draftsman with architectural training who had some very revolutionary ideas about mass entertainment. The neophyte showmen each had several concessions at the 1901 Pan-American Exposition in Buffalo. Dundy's Old Plantation was popular, but Thompson's illusionary Trip to the Moon was the hit of the fair. This wonderful attraction offered visitors an opportunity to enter a space ship; travel through simulated space; and land on a synthetic moon complete with rocky surface, the man in the moon seated on a throne, and midgets dressed as lunar inhabitants. As a souvenir, each visitor received an authentic piece of green cheese from the diminutive population. While many professed to find the lunar excursion "very realistic," they were soon brought back to earth by the midgets' rendition of "My Sweetheart's the Man in the Moon."

One of the visitors to the fair was George C. Tilyou, the successful owner and operator of Coney's Steeplechase Park. Tilyou offered Thompson and Dundy a contract to install A Trip to the Moon and their Giant See-Saw ride at Steeplechase for the 1902 season. The pair accepted the invitation. The attraction astounded visitors to Coney, and both the concessionaires and the park made a great deal of money. This success only whetted the appetites of Thompson and Dundy. At the close of the 1902 season, Paul Boyton sold them Sea Lion Park, which had operated at Coney since 1895. Tilyou kept the Giant See-Saw, but the Trip to the Moon went with Thompson and Dundy to their new park.

Most of Sea Lion Park was unimaginative, but its centerpiece was an exciting ride developed by Paul Boyton and named Shoot-the-Chutes. Sitting in flat-bottom boats, riders were hauled to the top of a steep incline. There the boats were turned and allowed to slide freely down a large chute that ended in a lagoon. Young men dressed as sailors stood in the boats and directed them back to the loading station.

Thompson and Dundy saw great possibilities for the Shoot-the-Chutes, but the remainder of Sea Lion Park they slated for destruction. During the winter of 1902-03, Dundy borrowed large sums of money from New York investors, while Thompson set about designing the most magnificent amusement park ever constructed. Fred Thompson had no formal architectural training, although he once worked as a draftsman in a Nashville architectural firm owned by his uncle, George Thompson. Even so, young Thompson won an award for his design of the Negro Building for the 1897 Tennessee Centennial Exposition. He also operated concessions at the Nashville fair and in 1898 opened additional concessions at the Trans-Mississippi and International Exposition in Omaha.

Buoyed by his financial and architectural successes at two expositions, Thompson moved to New York and studied under painters Kenyon Cox, Robert Blum, and Frederick Bridgman at the Art Students' League. By the time he met Skip Dundy in 1901, he was an imaginative architect who spurned traditional work to embrace the functional architecture of the world's fair and the amusement park.

Thompson's plan for the new park at Coney Island was well conceived and designed to stimulate the imagination, control the motion of the crowd, and reap the greatest of profits for the owners. In contrast to the world's fairs, Thompson had no inclination to educate the public. His only desire was to entertain and to convince visitors to spend their money. Referring to ballyhoos, Thompson stated, "All showmen use them, but I think I am one of the very few who have ventured to make architecture shout my wares."

Although familiar with classical architecture, Thompson abandoned all tradition and uniformity of design. As one historian has stated, Thompson used the conventional to create an unconventional park. To paraphrase Thompson, an architect of the amusement industry must be willing to decorate an Eastern minaret with Renaissance detail, or a Romanesque building with art nouveau trim. What this brilliant showman created has been described by Coney Island historian John F. Kasson as "Super-Saracenic or Oriental Orgasmic." Thompson freely, but carefully, combined every imaginable type of architecture. Classic Roman or baroque styles were blended with Indian, Arabic, Byzantine, Moorish, French, Japanese, Chinese, Italian, and Teutonic influences. Nowhere in the park were straight lines used. Each building seemed to both blend and contrast with the buildings around it. Everywhere, structures were enhanced with towers, minarets, archways, balconies, and elevated walkways. Bright colors were used throughout the park. For nighttime illumination, 250,000 colored lights were installed. At the very center of the park was Boyton's renovated Shoot-the-Chutes with its lagoon that reflected many of Luna's lights at twilight. The architecture of Luna Park was "designed confusion," but Thompson planned the confusion with attention

The Shoot-the-Chutes was the centerpiece of Coney's Luna and was duplicated in most other Luna Parks.
Author's Collection

In 1903, Luna Park illuminated the Coney Island sky with the greatest light show of the age.
Library of Congress

- 15 -

to every detail. If anyone tried to find meaning in Thompson's free use of griffins, gargoyles, and sea monsters, they were sadly disappointed. In fact, Thompson mocked the classical use of icons and installed mythical creatures wherever it served his plan to overwhelm the visitor.

In addition to the Shoot-the-Chutes and the transplanted Trip to the Moon, Thompson and Dundy invented or purchased a myriad of exotic attractions. Elephants performed on a platform suspended over the park's lagoon; and spread throughout the park's original twenty-two acres were the Chinese Theater, a Japanese garden, an Irish village, the Dutch Windmill Restaurant, a Venetian city, an Eskimo village, and even the Streets of Delhi. Every whimsical fantasy was recreated at Luna. Every human sense was stimulated by colors, sounds, and smells. Luna was like nothing the world had ever seen.

Luna opened on the evening of May 16, 1903, and the 45,000 who entered the park were stunned by the display of color and light. As one writer related a year later, "We were at the entrance, and the gates and the sight beyond filled us with profound amazement." He recalled that, "... first came the chariots where the tickets were sold ... and beyond them an enchanted, story-book land of trellises, columns, domes, minarets, lagoons, and lofty aerial flights." Just hours before opening the gates to Luna, Thompson and Dundy's personal cash reserves were down to $12 and they owed investors more than $700,000. By August, every penny had been repaid and the team of showmen were on their way to becoming wealthy. In 1904, four million people paid ten cents each to enter the mysterious land created at Coney. Despite the fact that Dundy was a notorious womanizer and Thompson

was an alcoholic, the partners kept each other in check. Unfortunately, Dundy died unexpectedly in 1907 and Thompson started drinking so heavily that he eventually lost control of both Luna Park and the New York Hippodrome, which had been constructed with the profits from Luna Park. Nevertheless, Thompson lived long enough to witness the emulation of his Luna Park concept from coast to coast and throughout the world. Had he been able to legally control and franchise the Luna Park idea, he might have died a wealthy man instead of a minor theatrical agent.

The symbol of Luna was the crescent moon and everyone assumed that the name Luna was related to the term lunar. This was a logical assumption since in Roman mythology Luna was the goddess of the moon. Thompson and Dundy, however, insisted that the park was actually named after Dundy's sister who lived in Des Moines. Whatever its origin, by 1905 the name Luna Park was known throughout the world and it was forever associated with the symbolic crescent moon.

The fame and mystique of Coney's Luna spread to all corners of the United States and the world. Scores of famous people visited the park, and John Philip Sousa, whose band performed there, wrote a song about Luna. In fact, Luna so impressed visitors to New York that one Cleveland lady who visited New York City in 1941 took note of only three landmarks: the Empire State Building, Horn & Hardart's automat, and Luna Park.

The spacious midway of Coney's Luna was designed to accommodate as many as four million visitors each season.
Cleveland Public Library

(above) At Hartford, Connecticut, the Luna Park Ferris Wheel was much larger, but still provided the riders with awnings for maximum comfort.
Hartford Public Library

(above left) The Whirlwind roller coaster at Schenectady's Luna Park. The architecture of the Whirlwind's station was very similar to that of the Jack Rabbit coaster at Cleveland's Luna.
Schnecetady County Historical Society

(left) The carousel at Hartford's Luna was a menagerie machine that featured horses and a variety of other animals.
Hartford Public Library

(below) Concert bands were featured attractions at every Luna Park, and a bandstand was the centerpiece of Hartford's park.
WKVL Amusement Research Library

LUNA PARKS ACROSS THE COUNTRY AND AROUND THE WORLD

As they had done with the roller coaster and other Coney Island innovations, showmen throughout the world decided that Luna Park represented a success story that could be profitably duplicated in any city with enough residents to support a park. Since Thompson and Dundy had no protection for either the name or the design of their park, enterprising men were free to build new Lunas wherever they chose. As a result, an uncounted number of Luna Parks rose between 1905 and about 1920. In the United States, Luna Parks opened in Chicago, Pittsburgh, Buffalo, Baltimore, Philadelphia, Atlantic City, Detroit, Denver, Indianapolis, Memphis, Cleveland, and Los Angeles. Others emerged at Charleston and Wheeling, West Virginia; San Jose, California; Schenectady, New York; Seattle, Washington; Scranton and Johnstown, Pennsylvania; Waterbury and Hartford, Connecticut; Mansfield, Ohio; and Houston, Texas. And still more sprang to life in Ardmore, Oklahoma; Bradford, Pennsylvania; Danville, Virginia; Greensboro, North Carolina; Miami, Florida; Millville, New Jersey; Ocean City, Maryland; Revere Beach, Massachusetts; Syracuse, and Sylvan Beach, New York.

Many of these parks survived only a few seasons, while others enjoyed a twenty-year life span. Some, like the operations at Washington, Buffalo and Seattle prospered until after World War I. Many went through name changes, and the Waterbury park later became Lakewood Park, while the Buffalo enterprise was renamed Carnival Court. At Schenectady, Luna Park opened about 1907 and was successively renamed Dolle's Park, Collonade Park, Palisades Park and Rexford Park, before finally closing in 1935.

LUNA PARK
MILLVILLE, N. J.
On the Shore of Union Lake
Opens Saturday, May 16th, 1925

Main Entrance

(above) The entrance to Luna Park at Millville, New Jersey, was featured in an advertisement for the 1925 season.
Steelman Photographics, Millville

(left) Most Luna Parks featured Ferris Wheels. This small version, at Millville's Luna Park, provided riders with protection from the sun.
Steelman Photographers, Millville

The tree-shaded bridge leading to the carousel and the midway at Charleston's Luna.
Harry M. Brawley Collection

The entrance to the park at Charleston, West Virginia, during construction.
Harry M. Brawley Collection

(left)   A line of concession stands being prepared for opening day at Charleston's Luna Park.
Harry M. Brawley Collection

(below)   The Royal Giant Dips coaster on the midway of the Charleston park. At the time, this was considered a large and daring ride.
Harry M. Brawley Collection

The many Luna Parks situated around the United States succeeded or failed for many reasons. The parks at Coney Island and Cleveland were, for the most part, managed well and survived beyond the end of the Luna Park mystique. Others were less fortunate. Pittsburgh's Luna was razed after only a few seasons when its owner became financially overextended. At Scranton, Luna Park was placed on the auction block after a fire in 1916 destroyed much of the park. And Chicago's Luna Park, located at Halsted and 52nd Street, may have failed because of its proximity to the odors of the Union Stockyards. Nevertheless, for a period of about fifteen years, the Luna Park movement was a franchise-like phenomenon that circled the globe. Just as the "golden arches" of McDonald's restaurants would be decades later, the crescent moon of Luna Park was a constant and reliable image that was recognized everywhere.

Each succeeding Luna Park emulated Thompson's Coney Island enterprise, while at the same time incorporating its own unique character and appearance. Cleveland's Luna Park was the largest of the offspring parks and the installation that most faithfully imitated the parent park. The park located at Mansfield, Ohio, bore the least resemblance to the original Luna. It was also the smallest of the world's many Luna Parks.

(above) Chicago's short lived Luna Park was located close to the stock yards.
Courtesy of James Abbate

(right) The park at Mansfield, Ohio, was probably the smallest of the Luna Parks in the United States.
Author's Collection

The Casino building at Mansfield's Luna survived long after the park closed.
Author's Collection

Geography and the tastes of the individual owners influenced many Lunas. Seattle's Luna Park, owned by carousel builder Charles Looff, was constructed on a pier jutting into Puget Sound. As a result, it was the only Luna Park with a midway surface made entirely of wooden planks. The Buffalo Luna, which was later re-named Carnival Court, featured a main entrance built of brick which imparted the cold look of an urban industrial edifice instead of the warmth of the Coney Island park. While most Lunas featured extravagant, towering entrances, the Scranton park had a very small, unassuming entrance. Once through the gate, visitors walked across a long bridge that spanned a ravine. Whatever their design, the string of Luna Parks that crossed the United States were second to none in their grandeur, color and uniqueness.

The Old Mill ride at Buffalo's Luna Park. Admission to the Old Mill was ten cents for adults and five cents for children.
Buffalo and Erie County Historical Society

Seattle's Luna Park, owned by carousel carver Charles Looff, was the only Luna built entirely on a pier.
Pemco Webster & Stevens Collection, Museum of History & Industry

Scranton's Luna Park was one of Ingersoll's chain of parks to open between 1905 and 1910.
Lackawanna Historical Society

The entrance to Scranton's Luna followed the Coney Island architectural theme, but on a much smaller scale. The crescent moon was associated with almost all Luna Parks throughout the world.

Jack Hiddlestone Collection

The Luna Park craze was not limited to the United States, however. Before World War I, Lunas illuminated the night skies in Canada, Mexico, the United Kingdom, Italy, France, Belgium, Austria, Germany, Hungary, Russia, Spain, Portugal, Australia, New Zealand, Argentina, Brazil, Cuba, Egypt, India, the Philippines, Japan, and Hawaii. Except for the United States, Australia was home to more Luna Parks than any other country. The first

Australian Luna opened in 1912 at St. Kilda. This installation was followed by parks at Glenelg, Sydney, Melbourne, Perth, and Brisbane. The total number of parks that bore the Luna name may never be known, but it is interesting to note that almost ninety years after the first Luna Park was conceived, parks of that name still exist in Australia and Italy. In addition, the name has been resurrected for a new park in Moscow's famous Gorki Park.

(left) Sydney's Luna Park also featured a huge face on an otherwise typical Luna entrance, circa 1950.
Martin Sharp Collection, Courtesy of Sam Marshall

The French version of the Luna theme, located at Paris, looked very much like the best of America's Luna Parks. The Paris park was also very successful, and lasted longer than many of the North American installations.
WKVL Amusement Research Library

Moulin Rouge
Clou des Luna Park Berlin 1911
System Rapp

(above) Germany's Luna Park was built in Berlin and, except for signs lettered in German, could easily be mistaken for any of America's larger Lunas.
WKVL Amusement Research Library

(below) Regardless of where the park was located, nighttime illumination was a hallmark of every Luna Park. Here, the influence of Coney Island's Luna is obvious at Barcelona, Spain. WKVL Amusement Research Library

BARCELONA — Saturno Parque (Aspecto nocturno

(above) In Australia, the traditional Luna Park entrance was modified to include a large, and sometimes forboding, face. This is Melbourne's park in 1924.

WKVL Amusement Reaearch Library

(middle left) Japan's Luna Park was still in operation during the 1930s. By that time, most American Luna Parks had already been closed and demolished.

Author's Collection

(middle right) Cairo's Luna Park appears to have been surrounded by poverty and debris. Nevertheless, it was a popular attraction.

WKVL Amusement Research Library

(right) This advertisement for Cairo's Luna Park (circa 1912) suggested that the park catered to both Europeans and Egyptians.

WKVL Amusement Research Library

MR. INGERSOLL

A large number of America's new Luna Parks were the products of Frederick Ingersoll, one of the most influential men in amusement park history. From his Pittsburgh offices, Ingersoll controlled a vast amusement empire. His influence was felt throughout the world. In the late 1890s, Ingersoll began inventing new amusement devices and improving on existing ones. He was particularly interested in the roller coaster and became one of America's premier coaster builders. In 1901, Ingersoll and E. E. Gregg formed the Ingersoll Construction Company for the purpose of installing rides and building entire parks. Since Gregg had been affiliated with the traction industry, many of the parks were built in conjunction with streetcar companies. In many cases, Ingersoll built the rides at his company's expense and paid the streetcar companies or park owners a percentage of the ride's revenues.

Ingersoll built many types of rides, but his most successful was the Figure Eight roller coaster. One of the early types of coasters, the Figure Eight featured small, four-passenger cars that ran in something like a wooden trough. Side friction boards running on either side of the track kept the cars on course. Ingersoll's chief designer and engineer, John A. Miller, contributed much to the success of the company, and by 1910 Miller was one of America's foremost roller coaster designers.

During 1901-02, Ingersoll built four Figure Eight coasters and in 1904 he reported the con-struction of twenty-three Figure Eight coasters, four Old Mill rides and thirty-six funhouses! During his active career, Ingersoll claimed to have built at least forty-four complete parks and three hundred roller coasters.

By 1904, Frederick Ingersoll was well aware of the success of Coney Island's Luna Park and embarked on a plan to construct similar parks throughout the country. Since the Ingersoll Construction Company did not have the resources to finance dozens of parks, Ingersoll and his talented salesman, Elwood Salsbury, generally selected suitable sites for parks and then sought local investors. Always, however, Ingersoll retained majority control of the new parks and often they opened under the banner of "Ingersoll's Luna Park."

Two of Ingersoll's greatest undertakings were the Luna Parks in Pittsburgh and Cleveland, both of which opened for the 1905 season. The Pittsburgh park was built at Grant Boulevard and Craig Street, very near the geographical center of the city. Always conscious of the importance of transportation, Ingersoll located the park so that ten streetcar lines passed the park's gates. Also, the park was built on a hill so that day or night, thousands of Pittsburgh residents were reminded of Luna's presence.

Pittsburgh's beautiful Luna flourished only until 1909, but Cleveland's Luna Park became a legendary amusement center that thrilled northern Ohioans for more than twenty-five years.

The design of Pittsburgh's Luna Park closely resembled that of the Coney Island park.
Library of Congress

"THE BRILLIANT ACHIEVEMENTS OF THE PAST ARE A GUARANTEE FOR THE FUTURE."

Pittsburg Luna Park

OPENS THE SECOND SEASON OF ITS TRIUMPHANT CAREER

May 7th, 1906

The Luna Park Co., of Pittsburg

FREDERICK INGERSOLL

President and General Manager

ADDRESS ALL COMMUNICATIONS TO THE
GENERAL OFFICE
307 Fourth Ave., Pittsburg, Pa.

Telephones: Bell 3363 Court; P. & A., 789 Main

A. S. BEYMER, Secretary and Treasurer   -   -   -   W. W. JIMISON, Local Manager

CHAPTER TWO

MR. INGERSOLL'S PARK

Ingersoll's Luna Parks were built simultaneously at Cleveland and Pittsburgh between the summer of 1904 and the spring of 1905. Ingersoll arrived in Cleveland in spring of 1904 and successfully interested a group of wealthy investors. The group was led by attorney Andrew Squire and included paving contractor Matthew F. Bramley, and stock brokers Mervin C. Harvey and Addison Hough. This group of men invested $300,000 in Ingersoll's scheme to build a park at Cleveland, and on August 23, 1904, the Ingersoll Amusement Company was incorporated. The profitable intent of the investors was somewhat hidden in the company's stated purpose: To provide "…the public with amusements of various kinds, educational and beneficial."

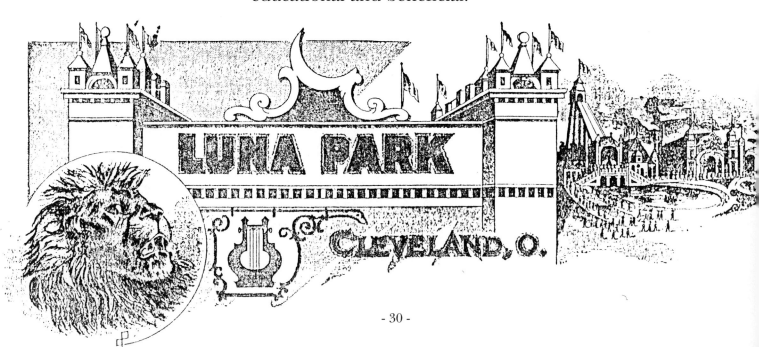

Ingersoll carefully selected Luna's location for its proximity to residential neighborhoods Cleveland's Luna and streetcar lines.
Author's Collection

THE SITE

At the time of incorporation, neither Ingersoll nor the investors had selected a site for Luna Park. The area to the east of Cleveland already had Euclid Beach Park. In addition, plans were underway for another park, White City on the Lake, to be built very near Euclid Beach. Ingersoll favored a location nearer to the center of Cleveland, preferably situated on a hill for maximum visibility, and immediately adjacent to one or more streetcar lines.

By fall, Ingersoll decided on a tract of about thirty-one acres of land located on a pleasant hill at the northeast corner of Woodhill Road and Woodland Avenue. The parcel of land had occasionally been used as a local picnic grounds and was served by streetcar lines that ran on both Woodhill and Woodland. In fact, by using transfers, park visitors would be able to reach Luna Park conveniently via every streetcar line in Cleveland.

Frederick Ingersoll (center) was the majority shareholder and creator of Cleveland's Luna Park. Elwood Salsbury (left) served as publicity manager and, later, as general manager of Luna.
Frederick Fried Archives

A Shoot-the-Chutes boat enters the lagoon after a fast trip down the Chutes hill. To the right, additional boats await passengers.
Library of Congress

Around the site was a quiet, newly developed residential community. Although predominantly Hungarian, the residents included an ethnic mixture of Germans, Bohemians, Polish, and a few Russians. Although the area remained ethnically mixed for many years, it eventually became one of the city's significant Italian-American neighborhoods. It was the ethnic composition of the streets that surrounded the park that gave Luna some of its unique character, charm, and cosmopolitan atmosphere.

The land selected for Luna Park was originally acquired by the Cleveland Trust Company, who sold it to Daniel R. Taylor. In late October, it was sold by Taylor to the Ingersoll Amusement Company. The terms of the sale specified a sale price of sixty thousand dollars at five percent interest. Interestingly, Taylor did not obtain clear title to the land until 1907, and Ingersoll never fully paid for the property.

THE FIRST BUILDINGS AND RIDES

With the land secured, Ingersoll ordered blueprints for the park and entered into contracts for various rides and attractions. Most of the rides were actually built by Ingersoll's Pittsburgh-based construction company, but the carousel was ordered from another Pittsburgh firm, the T. M. Harton Company. Theodore Harton engaged the talented Philadelphia wood carver Daniel C. Muller to create the animals and chariots for the Luna Park carousel. Like most of Harton's carousels, the Luna ride was a menagerie machine that featured not only horses, but lions, tigers, goats, deer, giraffes, and camels.

While Daniel Muller was creating his wonderful carousel carvings, construction began on Luna Park, and investors hoped for a May, 1905 opening date. The design of Luna faithfully emulated its Coney Island namesake and, in fact, was only a few acres smaller than the New York park. At the center of the park was a large lagoon. At one end of the lagoon was the huge inclined tower of the Shoot-the-Chutes. This incline extended for 350 feet and reached 135 feet. At the base of the Chutes a graceful bridge arched over the lagoon. Suspension bridges were built over the ravines that cut through part of the property, and for years after children would amuse themselves by causing the bridges to sway back and forth.

With opening day only two months away, Cleveland's Luna Park was still far from complete.
Carnegie Library of Pittsburgh, Courtesy of Paul Korol

The main entrance gate on Woodhill Road was a Cleveland landmark throughout the park's existence.
Author's Collection

The entrance to the park was almost an exact copy of the Ionic entrance to Coney's Luna. On the side facing Woodhill Road, an illuminated sign read "Ingersoll's Luna Park," and on the opposite side was another lighted sign that read "Good Night." This bold entrance was 150 feet wide and topped by a huge crescent moon and four Egyptian towers. Painted in bright white and gold, the entrance was illuminated at night by ten thousand electric lights. A broad, steep stairway led from Woodhill Road to the entrance, but later an escalator eased the walk to Luna's glittering gates.

Once through the gates, the offices of park manager W. O. Edmunds, publicity manager Elwood Salsbury, and advertising manager Harry Morrison were located conspicuously on the right. Next door was the Japanese Exposition. So colorful and elaborate was this exposition that manager Kurimaki Yasuturo stated, "You will find nothing of the kind so elaborate in Japan." The entire structure was of oriental design, and illuminated Japanese lanterns dangled from the

The Japanese Exposition was located just inside the main entrance and was considered the finest exposition of its type in the United States.
Author's Collection

roof. A dozen Geisha girls performed dances throughout the day, a tea garden offered warm refreshments, and a wide variety of oriental curios were sold by Japanese ladies dressed in authentic costumes.

Exotic costuming helped create Luna's international atmosphere.
Author's Collection

Photographer's flash powder illuminated tunnels of the Scenic River that were normally dimly lit and perfect for romantic interludes. Lackawanna Historical Society

Color and light were emphasized at the new park. The buildings of Luna were painted in an unending array of pinks, greens, yellows, oranges, blues, and purples. Since Luna was open until midnight, every structure was outlined in colored electric bulbs. In all, more than sixty thousand lamps prompted the advertising department to claim, "It's Never Dark at Luna Park." At night, when the park was in full illumination, the sky around Woodhill Road glowed with a bright aura that could been seen for miles.

Among the one hundred attractions of which Luna boasted were the largest Figure Eight roller coaster ever built; a giant slide in the shape of a shoe; and a Trip to Rockaway, a simulated ocean voyage that mechanically produced both storms and rolling seas. There was also Chateau Alphonse, a popular funhouse; an Electric Theater that recreated the eruption of Mt. Pelee many times daily; and Edisonia, where visitors enjoyed phonograph recordings and early moving pictures for just a penny.

A popular ride at the new park was Ingersoll's Scenic River. The facade of this ride featured a Dutch mill with an operating water wheel. A fleet of small boats carried patrons gently through nearly a mile of dark tunnels and buildings with lavish illuminated scenes from around the world. The obvious attraction the darkened tunnels held for young couples caused Luna's management to forbid hand holding on the ride, but this rule was honored more in the breach than in practice.

(below) The Old Shoe, a giant slide in the shape of a shoe, and a funhouse named Chateau Alfonse were two of Luna's favorite attractions in 1905. Library of Congress

The entrance to the Scenic River, Luna's version of the famous Old Mill ride.
Author's Collection

In the Caves of Capri, winds whistled from every direction and visitors meandered through a labyrinth of stalactites and stalagmites that reflected soft, shimmering lights. Like every attraction at Luna, the Caves of Capri provided the mystery and fantasy that was absent from everyday life in an industrial city.

The Casino, a great Moorish ballroom, was an airy structure measuring seventy-five feet by three hundred feet. This immense building was bordered by a series of parlors designed exclusively to assist the visiting mother with infants and young children. Here the park offered a day nursery, a large staff of children's maids, and a baby carriage livery. Luna was not designed as a child's park, but management did everything possible to help keep children occupied while their parents enjoyed the park's more mature offerings.

PLEASING THE PALATE

Like most parks, Luna provided inexpensive food and beverage services for its guests. Luna did not encourage picnic lunches, but it did offer a cool, scenic picnic grove located in a gently sloping valley beyond the steep ravine on the eastern end of the grounds. The secluded location was purposely selected, for park management hoped that most guests would buy their food at the park. Indeed, guests who did not bring picnic baskets found no shortage of food counters and refreshment stands. Luna's finest dining facility, the Cafe Napoleon, provided full à la carte service as well as cold draft beer. By June, the cafe had "...already become a favorite with the elite." Wines and liquors were never sold at Luna, but beer was always close at hand. However, Ingersoll was very discreet in the marketing of beer, and few beer signs were posted inside the park. Outside, however, a huge Gold Bond beer advertisement on the exterior of the fence greeted everyone entering the park from Woodhill Road. Those seeking a cold schooner of beer headed for the Roof Garden atop the massive Casino ballroom. From this high oasis, tables looked out over much of Cleveland. No tavern anywhere else in Cleveland could claim such a view.

Luna's original ballroom soon proved to be too small to handle the large crowds that flocked to the park. The ballroom was flanked by the entrance to the Scenic River and a refreshment stand that served soda waters, mineral waters and Italian ices.
Library of Congress

If the Cafe Napoleon and the Roof Garden catered to the local elite, several dozen food stands on the midway were established with the working-class visitor in mind. Near the white bridge that crossed the lagoon was a waffle stand that prepared thick, soft waffles similar to the Belgian waffles that would be introduced a half century later. Many Cleveland children remembered nibbling these waffles while seated on the lagoon bridge while Chutes boats rushed under them. On one side of the lagoon, the Old Taffy Shop offered Luna's famous cream candy in boxes that could easily be carried home on streetcars. Of course, there was also popcorn, fresh roasted peanuts, hot dogs, and roast beef served on buns dipped in rich gravy. While their families enjoyed the many confectionery treats, men wandered over to the cigar stand where five cent Ology cigars were the featured smoke.

Most unique among the food stands was the Candy Butcher Shop. Here was a butcher shop, complete with white-aproned attendants, that served sausages, hot dogs, ham sandwiches, pork chops, wedges of cheese, and various other food items. Each and every item, however, was made from a sweet coconut candy which was colored yellow for cheese, reddish brown for ham and other colors to simulate real meats and cheeses.

Glass cases were filled with these unique products, and from the ceiling were suspended long chains of candy sausage, linked together as if in a real meat market. Luna was expected to be different and exotic, and even the food concessions lived up to this image.

Charles P. Salen was among the most interesting food concession operators. In his public life, Salen became an important Cuyahoga County politician, initially serving as county clerk in 1878. He was later a delegate to the 1904 Democratic National Convention, a trusted lieutenant of mayor Tom L. Johnson, and an unsuccessful candidate for mayor. As Director of Public Works for the City of Cleveland, Salen constructed baseball diamonds, held ice carnivals, and sponsored skating races. Always interested in public recreation, he personally financed and built a skating rink near Edgewater Park. During the 1890s, Salen and Jake Mintz began operating food concessions. In addition to serving food at ballparks and other locations, they became important concessionaires at both

Luna Park and the short-lived Gordon Gardens. When Salen died in 1924, both the president and the general manager of Luna served as pallbearers.

OPENING DAY

All that was to become "The Land of Luna" came into being in just a little over six months. Well before Christmas of 1904, Ingersoll's plans for the park were finished and a crew of 500 carpenters and 100 electricians, plumbers, and painters worked through blizzards and rains to ready Luna for a May debut. Ingersoll was a busy man that winter. In addition to supervising construction of the parks at Cleveland and Pittsburgh, he also erected almost a dozen roller coasters throughout the East. In actuality, Cleveland's Luna was Ingersoll's thirty-fourth amusement park project, and construction proceeded with a military kind of organization and precision. With snow still on the ground, most of the major buildings neared completion.

While a battalion of tradesmen labored to finish Ingersoll's elaborate plans, publicity manager Elwood Salsbury planned a private showing for fifteen hundred invited guests on May 7. Among the first to step through Luna's great entrance were politicians, bankers, investors, major suppliers, the media, and several amusement park managers from Ohio and Pennsylvania. The attending reporter from the amusement industry's major periodical stated, "There is a certain gracefulness of outline, mingled with picturesqueness of design, which makes each and every individual part a pleasing sight and combines to make the ensemble unrivaled. For this Mr. Frederick Ingersoll is to be congratulated."

As opening day approached, advertising manager Harry Morrison saw to it that Cleveland was blanketed with more than ten thousand posters and billboards. The public clamored for an early view of Luna, and on Sunday, May 14, thousands gathered at the gate and asked to be admitted to the incomplete park. Turned away, they wandered around the park's fence hoping for a view of the unbelievable wonders they had been promised by the posters, the billboards, and newspapers reports. In an age when the advertising industry was still in its infancy, Luna's staff had engineered a true media blitz.

Prior to opening, Cleveland was flooded with Luna's promotional materials. Included was an elaborate brochure prepared by Ingersoll and publicity manager Elwood Salsbury.

James Abbate/National Amusement Park Historical Association

This ad for Luna Park's debut season appeared on May 18, 1905, in the Cleveland *Plain Dealer*.

Next to Chateau Alfonse was the Great Aerial Swing, a ride that simulated an airship flight. The cables that suspended the airship cars were decorated with strings of colored lights. At night, the swirling ride produced a dazzling display of color.
Library of Congress

Regardless of the park's state of readiness, Ingersoll announced May 18 as the opening day. Since Ingersoll was a veteran showman with numerous park openings behind him, he made sure that the gates opened on time. The day was sunny but cool, with temperatures reaching only the mid-fifties. Still, the crowds came, and one periodical reported that the crowd was, ". . . unequalled in size and enthusiasm by any gathering of its kind . . . ." A properly impressed local newspaper reporter stated that, "Such diversity of sights and amusements has never before been seen in the Forest City."

Those who attended Luna on opening day and throughout the coming seasons would recall an overwhelming feeling of enchantment. Never before or after would Northern Ohio experience an amusement park like Luna. As one visitor to Luna later stated, every other area park was dull and lifeless by comparison. Part of Luna's mystique was rooted in the fact that Ingersoll imitated Coney Island's Luna Park down to the smallest detail. All summer long there was never a moment of peace and quiet at Luna, only noise, motion and emotion. On opening day, visitors immediately realized that the activity at Luna never ceased. If the rides and games and shows were not enough, Ingersoll provided Gertrude Breton's spine-tingling free act wherein the young lady leaped a wide chasm in an automobile. And when Miss Breton was not leaping, William Barnes conducted Ingersoll's Red

On the evening before opening, several hundred workmen struggled to ready the midway for the next day. Even so, not all of Luna was ready. The Circus Ring was not completed until several days after opening day, and a number of rides were not ready to operate. The last ride to open, the Great Aerial Swing, did not make its debut at Luna until the middle of July.

The Circus Ring was located in front of the Night and Morning show and the small Art Parlor that featured a "Parisian Diorama."
Ohio Historical Society

Luna illuminations. Over 60,000 electric light bulbs provided one of the amusement park's most outstanding attributes.
Author's Collection

Cockade Band, a large musical organization of forty-five bandsmen and ten soloists.

When twilight arrived on opening day, more than sixty thousand colored lights were switched on and Luna emitted a glow that outshone the lights of downtown Cleveland. With the first illumination of the great new park, the curtain was raised on a twenty-five year span that proved to be one of the most amazing, exciting, and colorful eras in amusement park history.

After an enthusiastic opening day, Luna was launched on a non-stop, breathtaking season. Two days later, the first picnic outing arrived at Luna. The May Company, one of Cleveland's largest department stores, brought more than one thousand employees and families by automobile from the downtown store. Foot races, a catered dinner, and hours of free rides marked the first of thousands of group outings to come. A few weeks later, the National Association of Letter Carriers brought nineteen thousand to Luna, and the line for the Shoot-the-Chutes stretched for more than five hundred feet all day long.

Even when group outings were not booked, Luna's grounds were filled to capacity. On the first Sunday of operation, May 21, 1905, the local streetcar lines strained to bring more than fifty thousand people to the gates of Luna. The large crowds seldom slackened, despite all of the competition that Luna had to endure during its premiere season.

THE COMPETITION

The Cleveland of 1905 was a city bristling with entertainment facilities. The major vaudeville and stock company theaters included The Colonial, Keith's, the Empire, the Lyceum and the Cleveland. For less sophisticated crowds, the Blue Ribbon Girls could be seen at the "Home of Burlesque," the Star Theater. Of course, there was baseball at League Park; and Cleveland was an important stand for the larger circuses. During the summer of 1905, Ringling Brothers World's Greatest Show, Barnum & Bailey's Greatest Show on Earth, and the Hagenbeck-Wallace Circus all pitched their tents in Cleveland.

Luna's greatest competition came from the area's other amusement parks, as well as the city parks and beaches. In fact, just before Luna was built, the city took a serious interest in public parks. From a mere ninety-three acres of parks in 1890, the city's recreational holdings grew to fifteen hundred acres in 1905. These city parks provided free recreation, but failed to offer the commercial entertainments of the amusement parks. As a result, the commercial parks were Luna's most aggressive competition. Among these amusement parks, and far to the east of downtown Cleveland, was Euclid Beach Park. By the 1920s, Euclid Beach would become one of America's great parks, but between 1905 and the time of the First World War, it was but a minor

Willoughbeach Park, far to the east of Cleveland, was Luna Park's competitor for almost twenty years. Courtesy of the Lake County Historical Society

threat to the supremacy of Luna. On Cleveland's west side were Puritas Springs Park and Scenic Park. Located on the Rocky River near Lake Erie, Scenic Park claimed to have installed one of the first roller coasters in the area, but it was seldom able to attract crowds even half the size that frequented Luna and the other larger parks. Fifteen miles east of Public Square was Willoughbeach Park, a small but popular lakeside resort operated by the Cleveland, Painesville & Eastern electric railway. In addition to all of these, there was the rapidly expanding Cedar Point some sixty-five miles west of Cleveland. However, in 1905, Cedar Point was still strictly a summer resort and had not yet added its great amusement circle.

White City was a clean, attractive park. Its architecture, however, was not equal to the fairyland created at Luna. Library of Congress

(right) White City on the Lake opened in 1905 at East 140th Street and Lake Shore Boulevard. Library of Congress

The list of Luna's competitors was long and impressive and at the top of the list was White City on the Lake. In May of 1905, one local newspaper reported, "Not only has the amusement park lightening struck Cleveland hard this summer, but it struck twice, once out on the lake shore and again up in the hills to the southeast of the city…." The "lake shore" park referred to was the sparkling new White City on the Lake just west of Euclid Beach at East 140th Street and Lake Shore Boulevard , on the site of a smaller resort called Manhattan Beach. White City was a Coney Island-style park designed to rival Luna. Although its pristine white appearance lacked the color of Luna, White City was built on an extravagant scale. There was a Shoot-the-Chutes, a Scenic Railway, Sir Hiram Maxim's massive Flying Airships, infant incubators, a free circus, Bostock's famous wild animal show, and a ballroom that accommodated about three thousand dancers. The star of Bostock's animal show was Captain Jack Bonavita, the flamboyant animal trainer who lost an arm to a lion at Coney Island and was later killed by a bear. Just as Cleveland's Luna Park emulated Coney Island's Luna, White City was modelled after Coney Island's glittering Dreamland Park. Following Dreamland's example, several concessions were sold to popular showpeople. The Bump-the-Bumps ride was owned by vaudeville comedienne Marie Dressler, who helped publicize White City by appearing at her ride for a few days in June. If any park had the ability to compete with Luna, it was certainly White City.

The gate to White City was not as impressive as Luna's entry structure.   Library of Congress

The following breakout of attendance figures indicate where most Clevelanders spent July 4, 1905:

Luna Park	108,000
White City	85,000
Euclid Beach Park	80,000
City parks	60,000

Luna was so busy on its first big holiday that twelve thousand people paid admission to the park in just one hour between 5:00 p.m. and 6:00 p.m. As always, the holiday attractions at Luna were non-stop. Fairman's Concert Band was fresh from a successful engagement at Atlantic City. On the free act stage were Gorman's High Diving Horses and Sturant & Lavardo, the High Wire Marvels. By day, fireworks boomed from Professor Longsdorff's hot air balloons and at twilight, Pain's firework company provided a ten thousand dollar display unlike anything seen before in Cleveland. As the park claimed, the "Night Skies Jeweled with Stupendous SET PIECES and SHOWERS of FIRE."

LUNA ENTERTAINS

Throughout the 1905 season, entertainment in great variety became the theme of Luna . . . a theme that would last twenty-five seasons. Fireworks were displayed regularly, including a massive historical recreation called the Spectacle of Mt. Pelee. The outdoor free act stage presented a varied bill of acts that ranged from Herbert's Dog Circus to Hardy, the American Blondin. In the Scenitorium, a large theater that faced the Shoot-the-Chutes lagoon, motion pictures, vaudeville acts, singers, acrobats, and an endless line of chorus girls provided entertainment. Of the various offerings, vaudeville was second in importance only to concert bands. In 1905, vaudeville was immensely popular, and one contemporary observer noted, "There is a cheerful frivolity in vaudeville which makes it appeal to more people of widely divergent interests than does any other form of entertainment." Ingersoll recognized the importance of vaude-

ville and made it a centerpiece at Luna. It retained its place on the midway well into the 1920s.

Most important among Luna's entertainment offers, however, were the concert bands. Patrick Conway, while on a summer tour of amusement parks and resorts, brought his renowned Ithaca Band to Luna in July. Among the other bands to mount the stage during that first season were the Metropolitan Band of Italy,

INGERSOLL'S LUNA PARK, CLEVELAND, O.

Russo's Band, Robertson's Military Band, Frank Hruby's Great Western Band, Fanciulli's Band from New York, the Government Indian Band, Weber's Band, Callaghan's Marine Band, the Carnegie Library Band, and Ciricillo's Italian Boys' Band.

Luna's entertainment bill offered something for everyone. Because the park catered to the public's love of the exotic and even the forbidden, Luna was often controversial. The fact that the Catholic Mutual Benevolent Association brought twenty thousand people to its 1905 outing at Luna Park does not suggest that the clergy shared the public's enchantment with Luna.

In July, DeKreke's Mysterious Asia show, a big hit at the 1904 St. Louis World's Fair, came to Luna. The show featured musicians from Egypt, whirling dervishes, sword dancers and "hindoo" magicians. Most importantly, Mr. DeKreke employed native dancing girls in authentic, if revealing, costumes. During this season,

as well as in subsequent years, the churches of Cleveland took a dim view of Luna's dancing girls. The park patrons, however, held a different opinion and Luna's "girlie" shows were always packed with spectators.

Luna also came under fire because it served beer. Although the park never advertised its beer garden or served beer outside of selected areas, there was no question that beer was a major reason for Luna's popularity. When the Cleveland Christian Endeavor planned its outing at Luna for August 19, the organization's strong temperance leadership was apparently unaware of Luna's discreetly visible beer gardens. Once they became aware of Luna's beer garden, the CCE immediately announced to the newspapers that it could not hold an outing in a park where beer was served. Cancelling its contract with Luna, the group turned to beer-free Euclid Beach. This park was not as generous with prize money contributions as Luna had been, however, and all plans for the picnic were cancelled.

Pat Conway's Ithaca Band was the first of many famous concert bands to play at Luna.
DeWitt Historical Society

Frank Hruby was one of Cleveland's leading musicians and the director of a Luna Park favorite, the Great Western Band.
Frank M. Hruby

Dancing girls and beer drinking aside, the Ingersoll organization soon found itself embroiled in a more serious controversy with Cedar Point's powerful and vitriolic owner, George A. Boeckling. Ingersoll became a concessionaire at Cedar Point in 1902 and soon installed the Racer coaster, a carousel, and a funhouse. His contract with Boeckling ran through 1911, and Ingersoll had agreed to add more rides and attractions at Cedar Point each season. However, Ingersoll had not been very active at Cedar Point in recent seasons. Boeckling charged that his concessions were poorly managed and that the construction of Luna Park had drained Ingersoll's attentions and resources away from Cedar Point. As a result, Boeckling took legal action and asked that a receiver be appointed by the court to oversee Ingersoll's concessions. After a few weeks of tense conversation, Boeckling and Ingersoll came to an agreement. When Cedar Point opened its amusement circle in 1906, Ingersoll was a major ride operator. Thereafter, Boeckling and Ingersoll were cordial business associates and the Cedar Point amusement section proved profitable for both men.

For Fred Ingersoll, 1905 had been a landmark year. Despite his battle with Boeckling and a few local controversies, he opened two outstanding Luna Parks. Although Pittsburgh's park lasted only a few seasons, his Cleveland operation was among the greatest accomplishments of his very eventful life.

The final day of the 1905 season was on September 17. For the first time all season, the admission charge was waived and the gates were open from noon until midnight. The night before, a gala Confetti Carnival was held on the midway, and on closing day Duval, the Human Rocket, arrived directly from Coney Island's Dreamland Park and provided the season's final free act. When the gates finally closed at midnight, everyone in the city would agree that Luna had become "Cleveland's Colossal Fairyland."

ROBERTSON'S
FAMOUS
CONCERT
BAND.
KITAFUKU
Sensational Japanese
ACROBATS

LA BELLE MASQUE
SIX AMERICAN GIRLS

KANDY
KORNER
KOTTON
KANDY

CIGARS

Luna Park became so popular that even a rainy day could not keep crowds away. The entrance to the Scenic Railway, a roller coaster opened in 1906, is clearly visible.   Cleveland Public Library

CHAPTER THREE

CLEVELAND'S FAVORITE AMUSEMENT PARK

NEW AND IMPROVED

By the time Luna's buildings were shuttered for the winter, Fred Ingersoll was already busy planning for the 1906 season and beyond. Ingersoll, perhaps one of the most respected figures in the early amusement park industry, did not rest upon the laurels of the 1905 season. He knew, partially from personal experience, that successful amusement parks added new rides and attractions every season. As a result, each new season unveiled a slightly different, slightly more colorful, and always more interesting Luna.

(top) Luna was constantly being changed and improved. By the time this photo was taken, about 1910, the Night and Morning show had been converted to an entrance to the Concert Garden, the Art Parlor was a photo studio, and the theater to the left of the Shoot-the-Chutes served as a roller skating rink.   Cleveland Public Library

(middle left) A group of ladies about to enjoy the gentle dips of the Figure Eight coaster, about 1909. Cleveland Public Library

(bottom left) The Figure Eight was one of two roller coasters operating at Luna before 1910. Cleveland Public Library

(middle right) One of the bridges that spanned Luna's ravine gave spectators an excellent view of a Scenic Railway train as it rounded a curve and headed back toward the midway. Cleveland Public Library

(bottom right) The Scenic Railway, the largest of Luna's early roller coasters, was designed to take advantage of the park's ravines. Cleveland Public Library

Throughout the winter of 1905-06, carpenters were again kept busy inside the park's high plank fence. The major new attraction for the second season was the Scenic Railway roller coaster that utilized the natural hills and valleys of Luna's ravines. For an investment of forty thousand dollars, Ingersoll was able to build a roller coaster with a seventy-five foot first hill and several thousand feet of track. Although mild by the standards of roller coasters that would follow in a few years, the Scenic Railway was the most exciting ride Clevelanders had ever seen. For Ingersoll the new Scenic Railway provided several benefits: his most successful park had a major new ride that would result in personal profits and his own Pittsburgh construction firm handled both the design and construction.

Also new for 1906 was an incubator facility for premature babies, Okuni Sami and the Flying Lady levitation show, Barlow's

Hippodrome Elephants, and the spectacular Vesuvius fireworks exhibitions. A year later, Ingersoll installed a Ferris Wheel and an unusual new ride called the Rainbow Dips. Somewhat similar to a double Ferris Wheel, the Rainbow Dips was one of the earliest rides to provide multi-axis movement. He also expanded the ballroom, operated it seven nights a week, and dubbed it the "Greatest Ballroom in Ohio." Atlantic City-style rolling chairs were added to the midway for those who enjoyed touring Luna in comfort, and several thousand more incandescent lights were installed in a park already ablaze with colored lighting. By 1907, Ingersoll and Elwood Salsbury, now the park manager, boasted that Luna offered visitors more than one hundred tantalizing attractions.

The Rainbow Dips was an unusual ride that lasted only a few seasons at Luna. The Rainbow Dips proved difficult to maintain and had limited earning capacity. These two views show the rides location and details of design.

Author's Collection/Richard F. Hershey Collection

It was fortunate that the Concert Garden was expanded in 1908, for the acclaimed Liberati played to standing-room-only crowds. Unlike Sousa, who played whatever the crowd requested, even if it was "Turkey in the Straw", Liberati revered classical and operatic scores. His own marches, like the "Kansas City Star" and the "Al Koran March" appeared on some programs, but scenes from *Faust, LaGioconda,* and *Cavalleria Rusticana* were more common. Twice a day, Liberati's Band mounted the stage in full uniform, while his beautifully-costumed opera company performed arias and duets while in full costume.

Despite the heavy classical repertoire of Liberati, the Concert Garden was an overwhelming success. Those who came to hear Liberati and the other bands were described as cosmopolitan. It was a truly democratic mixing of the classes, where "...women of fashion are seated on the same bench with secretaries and charwomen." At a typical afternoon or evening concert, "More than a dozen nationalities are represented. Rich and poor are found sitting side by side."

ON WITH THE SHOW – VAUDEVILLE AND CIRCUS ACTS

The intermingling of rich and the poor was not the only characteristic that gave Luna its unique flavor and spirit. The blending of numerous types of shows and attractions revealed the eclectic nature of the park. The free acts and the numerous stage shows that Luna offered established for the park an exotic charm that was never matched by Euclid Beach, White City, or any of the other area parks.

The circus-type acts that included everything from acrobats to Hardy, the King of the Wire and conqueror of Niagara Falls, were always major attractions. Typical of Luna's colorful performers was A. Wilson Hartley Snow who, depending upon the engagement, was billed as Dr. Hartley Snow, Sequah, or Okuni Sami. After working with William F. Cody, travelling with circuses, and taking his own acts around the world, Snow met J. B. "Benny" Morris at Coney Island. Morris had a very popular levitation act called the Flying Lady at Dreamland Park. Snow quickly became associated with Morris and took the Flying Lady on a tour of eastern and midwestern parks. Dressed in "hindoo" garb and headlined as Okuni Sami, Snow brought the act to Luna in 1906 and, in nineteen weeks, claimed $12,500 in profits. During the following seasons he played unsuccessful dates at parks in Brooklyn, Pittsburgh, and Buffalo, only to return to Luna in 1909 for a profitable eight-week engagement.

Sequah (a stage name used by A. Wilson Hartley Snow) was typical of the vaudeville and circus performers engaged by Luna's management.
Mrs. Boyd Berry

On a typically busy summer afternoon, a crowd begins to gather around the Circus Ring, anxiously awaiting the next performance.
Norman Petri Collection, Courtesy of Lee O. Bush

Cleveland audiences seemed to appreciate unique acts, and as news of the success of performers like Snow spread throughout the amusement industry, Luna's managers were besieged by hopeful performers seeking contracts. Often the acts were death-defying and thrilling, but some were too outlandish even for Luna. One act that was not booked in 1910 was a troupe of wire walkers who proposed walking on barbed wire stretched from the main gate to the Shoot-the-Chutes tower!

Okuni Sami (another stage name for Snow) performed his Flying Lady act at Luna in 1906 and again in 1909.   Mrs. Boyd Berry

Not surprisingly, among the shows that were consistently booked were touring companies featuring scantily-clad dancers. Although these shows were never immoral, they straddled the fence between proper and improper. In so doing, the shows drew applause from thousands of spectators and arrows of disapproval from scores of clergymen.

Generally, Luna's sexier shows were thinly veiled in respectability. In 1908, when Max Trostler's show, *In Cupid's Garden,* arrived after a popular run at Chicago's White City, it was billed as "artistic." Indeed, the show included operatic soloists and even a ballerina, Viola Napp. But the centerpiece of the show was a chorus line of thirty beautiful dancers. A season later, Luna's Plaza Theater hosted Arthur Nelson's five-scene production billed as an automobile drama. Again, the main draw of the show was a "Broadway Beauty Chorus" of thirty girls. By 1910, there were at least three girlie shows on Luna's midway, including the Jolly Girls at the Plaza Theater and fifty alleged Eskimo girls who comprised the Arcticia show. The big show of that year, however, was *Creation,* which came to Cleveland directly from the Palace Theater in London. The focal point of this illusion show was a group of shapely girls who first appeared on stage as stone statuary, evolved into living, dancing ladies, and in the finale, returned to a marble-like state.

The northeastern corner of the midway about 1908. The Plaza Theater is located between the Rifle Range and the carousel building, with the Shoot-the-Chutes entrance in the foreground.   Courtesy of Bruce Young

with Pawnee Bill's Wild West, played the old circus grounds on Scranton Road. Buffalo Bill was still the king of the wild west shows and nothing that Luna could offer compared with Bill Cody's show. Bill's announcement that this was to be his final season with the show drew large crowds to the circus grounds, but the old trouper continued to perform until his death some years later.

If animal shows, baby incubators and wild west extravaganzas brought people to Luna during the day, fireworks kept the crowds on the midway until late at night. In 1910, the park's board of directors authorized twenty thousand dollars for fireworks and New York's Sig Rozzi was engaged to provide displays on Mondays, Wednesdays and Saturdays. On May 18, a fabulous display celebrated the return of Halley's Comet to the skies over Cleveland. A huge, thirty-foot-high set piece that took six weeks to construct was moved to the center of the lagoon and the Shoot-the-Chutes was temporarily closed. A crew of eighteen men prepared the piece for ignition and at nine o'clock, the Halley's Comet display erupted with so much fire that its glow could be seen throughout most of Cleveland.

Fred Ingersoll soon realized that Luna was Cleveland's premier amusement park and its offering far exceeded those of the more sedate and restrictive Euclid Beach. However, Euclid Beach did have Lake Erie and a marvelous bathing beach to attract visitors on hot August days. The fact that Luna was land-bound did not stop Ingersoll from offering swimming. During the spring of 1910, the park company invested ten thousand dollars in the construction of Lake Luna. Part of the ravine was dammed, a concrete floor was poured, and sand was spread over the concrete before the lake was filled with water. Wading was permitted in the shallow end of Lake Luna, while diving, water polo, and swimming races were encouraged in the deeper end. A bathhouse was built, and a bathing suit rental operation opened. People planning to swim in Lake Luna were cautioned to arrive early, however, for there were seldom enough bathing suits to meet the demand on a sultry afternoon.

LUNA TAKES OFF – HIGH LEVEL ENTERTAINMENT

When Luna's gates first opened in 1905, it had been less than two years since the Wright Brothers' first flight at Kitty Hawk. Everyone was interested in flight, and although no airplanes were yet available for public exhibitions, hydrogen-filled airships were just as exciting. Luna was quick to take advantage of the public's interest and the first week of June, 1906 was declared "Airship Week" at Luna. The park signed a contract with aeronauts Lincoln Beachey and A. Roy Knabenshue. Beachey, who recently completed an engagement at the Portland Exposition, was already a popular flier and soon became even more famous for his exploits in fixed-wing aircraft. By the time of a fatal crash, he was one of America's best-known aviators. Both men made daily flights over Cleveland from their Luna Park base in Knabenshue's dirigible. Knabenshue was to arrive on June 3, but Beachey began making test flights several days earlier. Three thousand spectators turned out to watch Beachey's initial flight, but on his second flight they saw more than expected. Five hundred feet over Luna, a bamboo support snapped and a huge hole was torn in the fabric bag that contained the gas. The damaged airship barely cleared the Shoot-the-Chutes tower and landed awkwardly in an open field near the park.

Aeronaut A. Ray Knabenshue in flight, 1906.   Smithsonian Institution

Lincoln Beachey was the most famous dirigible pilot to exhibit his flying skills at Luna. After his 1906 engagement at Luna, he began flying fixed-wing aircraft and died in a plane crash.

Smithsonian Institution

A crowd gathers around the airship piloted by Lincoln Beachey.
Cleveland Press Collection,
Cleveland State University

For the next few seasons, Luna's manager paid little attention to aviation as an attraction. By 1910, however, Luna emerged as one of the nation's centers for both aircraft and dirigible flight. In fact, Luna became so well known for its aerial exhibits that would-be aviators without aircraft asked the park's management for funds to construct their machines. In return, they promised exhibition flights that would pack the park with spectators.

The 1910 season opened with German aeronaut Adolph Wullman's "War Balloon" ascensions. But Wullman was plagued with problems from the beginning. In his act, the balloon was to rise to about one thousand feet, at which time the aeronaut would parachute into the park and the balloon would sink slowly to earth. On May 15, eighteen thousand spectators came to see

Wullman, but the wind caught his parachute and he landed on a factory roof thirty city blocks from the park. A week later, Wullman lost control of the balloon, which dragged him through the trees and inflicted many painful cuts and bruises. If the act was dangerous for Wullman, it was also risky for spectators. On May 18, a man watching the balloon from the street outside the park gate was run down and killed by a horse!

Wullman's aerial problems and attendant dangers did not affect Luna's new devotion to flight. By August, Frank Goodale, a twenty-one-year-old pilot, arrived at Luna with his dirigible. Goodale in a dirigible and J. O. Gill, who made a triple parachute drop from a balloon, kept the people in the park and in the streets around Woodland Avenue looking skyward throughout the month.

Late in August, the aeronauts were joined by the first fixed-wing aircraft to attempt a flight from the park. C. W. Cain, learning of Glenn Curtiss' plan to fly from Euclid Beach to Cedar

The picnic grounds provided the setting for company and family gatherings.
Author's Collection

Point in late August, hoped to precede Curtiss as the first man to pilot an aircraft in Cleveland. On August 27, Cain's associate, R. J. Linley, started the plane's engine for a test flight. As he bumped across Luna's athletic field the craft rose about a foot into the air. Linley lost control and slammed into Luna's tall wooden fence. Viewing the wreckage, Cain noted that the plane could be repaired, but not in time to be the first pilot over Cleveland. A few days later, Curtiss made his record breaking flight from Euclid Beach to Cedar Point while Cain was grounded at Luna Park.

The only problem with balloons, dirigibles, and airplanes was that spectators could see them just as well from outside the park as from the midway. In addition, aerial mishaps were causing many delayed and cancelled flights. In an attempt to eliminate some of the problems of aerial exhibitions, while holding the public's interest, Luna opened an imaginative show called The Battle in the Clouds on July 18, 1910.

Part of the picnic grounds were converted to an arena, and in the center of the seating sections a miniature landscape was created. Duplicated in miniature were airports, wireless towers, aerial tramways, military installations and assorted buildings. After the spectators were settled in their seats, a warning was sounded and the crowd was advised that enemy airships were approaching. Dirigibles moved overhead on almost invisible wires; soon anti-aircraft batteries began firing at the airships. Several airships fell

as parachutes emerged from them and other airships dropped bombs on the city. Suddenly, an ammunition magazine exploded, followed by a ten-minute blasting by fireworks. Finally, the airships landed and the invaders took control of the city. After the show, spectators were encouraged to examine the little airships that had caused so much destruction on the miniature battlefield. None of the amazed onlookers realized that a deadly, full-sized version of aerial warfare would occur in France only four or five years later.

The Battle in the Clouds was such an instant success that people planning to attend the show were urged to purchase tickets in advance at Deutsch's downtown pharmacy. Prices were high for 1910. At a time when most shows at Luna were five cents or ten cents, tickets to The Battle in the Clouds cost from fifty cents to a dollar. But the high cost of the show did not deter the crowds. On one Tuesday night in July, 11,453 spectators paid to see the loud and colorful show.

OUTINGS

The popularity of Luna Park, which actually seemed to increase each year, attracted many groups that held annual summer outings. Of the hundreds of groups that scheduled summer picnics at Luna, many moved their events to Luna from White City, Euclid Beach or Silver Lake Park near Akron. During a typical month, August of 1908, every day was booked with at least one organized outing.

Bailey's department store moved its picnic to Luna, as did the Al Koran Shrine, who brought 20,000 to 1906's Shrine Day. The Shriners began their day with a parade in downtown Cleveland, followed by an automobile caravan to the park. Throughout the day, the Arab Patrol entertained with precision military drills and games were held for the children at the athletic field. One of the youngest contestants, five-year-old Virginia Hahn, was awarded a beautiful French bisque doll for her speed in a foot race. Another picnic that featured an automobile caravan was Baker Auto Day. Although this was an employee event, the Baker company used the outing as an excuse to showcase their vehicles by parading one hundred cars through the streets of Cleveland on their way to the park.

Political and labor organizations always found Luna ideal for outings that combined politics and recreation. The Republicans used Luna for years, each year bringing important national and local politicians to the podium of Luna's stage. A typical Republican outing occurred in 1906 when Sherburn Becker, the mayor of Milwaukee, and future president Warren G. Harding were key speakers. Not to be outdone, the Democrats began picnics at Luna in 1908, with Cleveland mayor Tom L. Johnson, then in the midst of a fight to control Cleveland's traction industry, as the honored guest. Then, in 1909, the Socialists booked an event that drew twelve thousand to hear controversial Socialist and historian Algie M. Simons. Of course, there was also Labor Day. This traditional finale to the summer season provided an excellent opportunity for both politicians and labor leaders to preach their gospel to a friendly and interested crowd. Labor Day of 1906 began with one hundred thousand people lining the downtown streets for a parade. Later in the day, fifty thousand crowded Luna to hear an address by James Duncan, vice president of the American Federation of Labor. Although the owners of Luna Park were mostly Republicans and certainly not friendly to the idea of organized labor, it was clear that any group with adequate funds could find a warm welcome at Luna.

Nationality days, like the German Singing Society Day and the Hungarian Festival, were always popular, as were days sponsored by retailers located throughout the city. The Strauss-Miller Company, who claimed to be Ohio's largest complete home furnisher, distributed tickets to its customers for free admission to the park plus a certain number of free rides and attractions. When fifteen hundred grocers closed their stores on June 22, 1910, forty thousand Clevelanders were their guests for free rides and a chance to win prizes in potato races, three-legged races, pie eating contests, and bag races. When the butchers held their annual event at Luna, a ten-cent ticket entitled twelve thousand people to admission and free roast beef sandwiches. During their picnic, the butchers of Cleveland roasted oxen in an outdoor pit and, before the day was over, served sixty thousand sandwiches.

While Luna's owners were certainly profit-oriented businessmen, they also had a philanthropic side. Each season, the park's management invited several orphanages to be guests of the park. Groups of more than five hundred orphans came to Luna for a day and manager Salsbury provided free admission, rides, an Indian show, popcorn, ice cream, candy, and peanuts. Charitable motives aside, such events provided excellent publicity coverage for the park in the local newspapers.

ON THE RIGHT TRACK – TROLLEYS

For every group that came to Luna Park before 1910, the convenience of streetcars that stopped at the park gates was an important consideration. Since the majority of Clevelanders did not yet own automobiles, public transportation had a great deal to do with the success of the park. In fact, Luna had a significant advantage over Euclid Beach because of its proximity to Cleveland's population centers and the major streetcar lines. Because Euclid Beach was far to the east of town, riders on some streetcar routes spent at least seventy-five minutes on cars bound for the Beach. By comparison, the longest ride to Luna was thirty-five minutes and the shortest, five minutes. The average Clevelander took forty-six minutes to travel to Euclid Beach, but only nineteen to reach Luna. In addition, it cost less to ride to Luna. In 1910, fares to Euclid Beach were ten cents, while those to Luna were only three cents.

For the Cleveland Electric Railway Company, Luna, Euclid Beach, and White City meant heavy summertime traffic. Each spring, the company hired nearly five hundred additional motormen and conductors to augment its regular force of two thousand operators. Throughout the city, summer cars bound for Luna carried a blue,

The park opened on schedule and the new Quincy Line provided reasonable, if somewhat delayed, service. Many Clevelanders feared violence, however, and only about five thousand people arrived at park on streetcars. No incidents were reported, but the mood was tense at Luna throughout the day. Rumors that streetcars were going to be dynamited spread through the park and about 10:00 p.m., false rumors that violence had erupted caused a mad rush to the waiting streetcars. No violence actually occurred, the traction officials handled the crowd efficiently, and concerns over the 1908 street railway strike came to a peaceful end.

THE COMPETITION PERSISTS

As popular as Luna was between 1905 and 1910, it was never without serious and capable competition. Even though Euclid Beach did not eclipse Luna until after the World War, the Humphrey family started aggressively competing with Luna about 1907. That year the Humphreys spent $140,000 for one of the largest Scenic Railways in the country and for extensive campground expansion. That same year, the steamship *Eastland* began making a daily run from Cleveland to Cedar Point. Although Cedar Point had always been primarily a summer resort, in 1906 it entered the amusement park business with the construction of a large new amusement circle. Interestingly, Fred Ingersoll was one of Cedar Point's major ride concessionaires. There was also Silver Lake Park near Akron, a pleasant resort operated by staunch Methodists who never operated their park on Sundays. Despite the distance from Cleveland to Silver Lake, the popular park was well served by both railroads and electric railways. As a result, many Clevelanders visited Silver Lake each summer.

crescent-shaped sign bearing the words "Luna Park" in the front window.

During Luna's first season, the Scovill Line ran from Public Square to the Luna Park Loop and provided service until four o'clock each morning. However, by 1906, the Scovill Line had ceased to exist and the Woodland Avenue Line became the primary transportation artery to the park. Accordingly, Ingersoll built an additional entrance to the park on Woodland Avenue and announced that cars would stop at Luna every two minutes, and every minute on busy days. When the new East 105th Street Line opened in 1906, the company reminded Clevelanders that every streetcar route in Cleveland now connected with the park via the East 105th Street Line. Using transfers, a rider could travel to the park from anywhere in the city for three cents.

Streetcar transportation was so important to both Luna and Euclid Beach that when a violent streetcar strike hit Cleveland just days before the opening of the 1908 season, park management reacted quickly. Following rumors that striking traction workers would cut the overhead wires leading to Luna on opening day, park manager Salsbury asked for a conference with Fred Kohler, Cleveland's legendary chief of police. Chief Kohler assigned a captain, fifty officers and a number of patrol cars to guard the tracks approaching the park. If necessary, Kohler boomed, he would line the streetcar tracks leading to Luna with Cleveland policemen.

Willoughbeach, another "dry" park, was also an active competitor of Luna, as was a newcomer, Lincoln Park (formerly Scenic Park). Opened in 1906 on the banks of the Rocky River, Lincoln Park featured a Scenic Railway, a Circle Swing, the Japanese Village, the Egyptian Hall, and other attractions similar to Luna's.

A Cleveland streetcar on the Woodland Avenue Line displays Luna's crescent-shaped sign in the front window.

Author's Collection

Avon Beach Park was many miles west of Cleveland. Because of electric railways, however, it provided Luna with some minor competition around 1910.

Author's collection

Lincoln Park proclaimed more free attractions than all of the other area parks combined. But, despite the convenience of streetcar service, Lincoln Park was a short-lived enterprise.

Luna's major competition was still White City on the Lake, but White City seems to have been one of the most unlucky parks in history. The park enjoyed a successful 1905 season and prepared to reopen on May 26, 1906. Improvements had been made to White City, including a water intake in Lake Erie that provided a constant flow of fresh water to the Shoot-the-Chutes lagoon.

On the day before opening, workmen were busy applying tar to the boat channel in the Old Mill when a torch ignited the tar. Within two hours, everything but the Scenic Railway had been destroyed by fire. Gone were thirty concession buildings, the cafe, the Shoot-the-Chutes, the power house, the ballroom, and the unoccupied infant incubators. Bostock's menagerie buildings were also destroyed, but fortunately the animals had not yet arrived for the season. Even with losses of $200,000 and an insurance policy covering only $60,000, president E. C. Boyce vowed to rebuild White City. The White City fire had an interesting effect on Luna. Fearing a similar conflagration, Ingersoll formed a park fire department and hired a full-time fire chief. The department's occasional fire drills proved an exciting spectacle for park visitors and provided an excellent opportunity for publicity.

White City began to rebuild and the new park opened late in June, 1907. A number of the major attractions were reconstructed and, at the same time, the park company abolished the sale of alcoholic beverages. The architecture of the resurrected park was attractive and the midway included a dance hall, a restaurant, an Indian Village, wild animal shows, and a sea lion exhibit in the lagoon that had previously served the fire-ravaged Shoot-the-Chutes.

In keeping with White City's unlucky tradition, the rebuilt park was open only about a month when it was struck by a violent wind storm that tore roofs loose, flattened tents, and tossed ticket booths fifty feet. The scenery for Pain's *Pompeii* firework show collapsed and White City was again in ruins. Undeterred, the damage was again repaired and White City reopened for what remained of a very short season.

In 1908, White City opened with a free gate to compete with nearby Euclid Beach. The season was disappointing, however, and the park was sold to new owners who opened the facility in 1909 as Cleveland Beach Park. The park had about fifteen rides, including a carousel, the old Scenic Railway and the Mystic River. It also offered "polite" vaudeville, band concerts, Pain's fireworks and a bear den that was home to ten polar bears. Cleveland Beach drew good crowds, but the initial popularity of the 1905 White City was never equalled, and the operation soon faded from the amusement park scene. From 1910 on, the competition for Cleveland's amusement dollar was primarily a battle between the very proper Euclid Beach and the sentimental favorite, Luna Park.

In the spring of 1909, a writer for the Cleveland *Leader* summarized what local residents already knew about Luna Park: "Luna in brief, is the one place where a man feels at liberty to parade his emotions in their shirt sleeves and where woman can cut the staylaces of her feelings and enjoy herself untrammeled." All of this was true, providing that the writer was referring to white men and women. For black Clevelanders, Luna evoked very different images.

Very few early American amusement parks welcomed black customers. In the North, many parks simply denied blacks entry; in the South, cities like New Orleans had one park reserved exclusively for whites and another for blacks. Segregation was no stranger to Cleveland area amusement parks and as early as 1896, blacks were forbidden to enter Euclid Beach's dance pavilion. As both Euclid Beach and Luna Park grew, each became more sensitive to segregation and by 1910 both parks had all but totally excluded blacks. At Luna, blacks were simply not admitted, except on a very few Jim Crow days scheduled for selected weekdays or after the close of the regular season. Surprisingly, in 1910, the Cleveland Association of Colored Men chose Luna for their first annual Emancipation Day. The event was very successful, and people came from as far away as Sandusky, Elyria, and Ashtabula for the annual outing. Although patrons of Emancipation Day were free to enjoy the midway concessions and rides, they were not welcome to swim in Luna Lake. Ironically, the facility was closed on Emancipation Day. The park insisted that the swimming area was closed

only for necessary maintenance, but when it happened each year the intent was obvious. Finally, by 1919 the Emancipation Day committee tired of management's racial policies and moved the event to Puritas Springs Park. The new location was never as popular as Luna, and within a few years the traditional event was suspended. Segregation policies remained in effect at Luna until the day the park closed.

Between 1905 and 1910, Luna was an extremely popular and successful business venture. In fact, a measure of its popularity is revealed in a note written by an unidentified Clevelander in June of 1906: "Visited fair Luna on Saturday evening for the second time this season. Had a great time. Will go again next Saturday Evening when the Protective Home Circle hold their picnic." Crowds were consistently large, and at no time did Ingersoll stop making improvements to the park. However, Fred Ingersoll was having personal financial difficulties. After building numerous parks and countless rides, the great showman was financially over-extended. By 1908, Ingersoll was in danger of bankruptcy and was finding it impossible to service his debt. A year later, the gravity of Ingersoll's situation became clear when Pittsburgh's Luna Park was unexpectedly closed and razed.

The immediate effect of Ingersoll's financial stress on Cleveland's Luna was unclear. In fact, few Clevelanders even knew of the Pennsylvanian's plight. However, late in 1908, the Ingersoll Amusement Company ceased making payments to the owner of the park land, Daniel R. Taylor. Still owing $35,500 plus five percent interest,

Taylor was unable to secure payments. In October of 1909 he sold the property to the Garfield Savings Bank. In the meantime, rumors suggested that Luna Park would be moved to a new location somewhere in the Cleveland area. Once the Ingersoll Amusement Company resumed payments to the bank, however, the rumors ended and plans for the 1910 season were launched.

The 1909 season unquestionably was affected by Ingersoll's personal troubles. Uncertainty about the park's future delayed plans for the season until the last minute. In April, manager Elwood Salsbury was still searching for a concessionaire to operate the fifteen hundred seat theater and for others to install shows and games of all kinds. The park opened late that season. Operations did not begin until late in May. Although Euclid Beach remained open until October 3, Luna quietly closed on September 10.

The 1910 season resulted in some improvements in the company's financial stability, and Ingersoll approved the construction of the tree-shaded Cafe Gardens, an English tea garden situated near the lagoons. Also new for 1910 was the Human Dry Cleaner, a revolving barrel that allowed men and women to become hopelessly and intimately entangled. To the average observer, Luna looked a little cleaner, a little fresher and a little whiter than usual. But Luna's sparkle was purely superficial as Fred Ingersoll was on the verge of financial collapse. Luna Park and its founder were about to go their separate ways and, for Luna, a new and exciting era was about to be born.

Luna Park, **Cleveland** *Sixth City*

CHAPTER FOUR

A DECADE OF GROWTH

MR. INGERSOLL SAYS "GOODBYE"

Because Fred Ingersoll was the Ingersoll Amusement Company's majority shareholder, the future of Luna Park was very much tied to Ingersoll's personal finances. Despite his vast amusement empire, Ingersoll's entertainment network was founded on bank loans and promissory notes. In fact, Ingersoll was already financially overextended by the time the Cleveland and Pittsburgh Luna Parks opened in 1905. By issuing many promissory notes, Ingersoll deferred scores of payments until 1907. As 1907 came to an end, however, he had made no effort to service his debts.

In January of 1908, four creditors petitioned the United States District Court in Pittsburgh and attempted to force Ingersoll into involuntary bankruptcy. Leading the creditor group was Gustav A. Dentzel, a respected Philadelphia carousel builder who supplied carousels to Ingersoll in 1905 for his Luna Parks at Scranton, Pennsylvania, and Washington, D.C. Dentzel held notes for seventy-five hundred dollars that he never to collected.

Ingersoll admitted his debt to Dentzel and one other creditor, but denied other debts, as well as the charge that he had given preferential treatment to certain creditors by improperly transferring park company stock in lieu of payments. Ingersoll requested and received a trial by jury. In June of 1908, this jury found that the creditors had not proved their case and Ingersoll was judged legally solvent.

The satisfaction this decision may have given Ingersoll was short-lived. By late 1910, 133 creditors were clamoring for $179,668.94 in debts that Ingersoll incurred between 1905 and 1908.

Anticipating legal action, Ingersoll made plans to dispose of his shares of stock in various parks, including Cleveland's Luna (excluding 210 shares of Ingersoll Amusement Company stock securing a debt to a Pittsburgh company). The Cleveland park's shareholders also anticipated Ingersoll's financial demise and on February 24, 1911, formed the Luna Park

Matthew F. Bramley, who acquired Luna Park in 1911, was a successful businessman with the heart of a showman.
Cleveland Public Library

Amusement Company. The following month, the board of directors of the Ingersoll Amusement Company authorized the sale of Luna Park to the new company. The sale price was never officially revealed, but it was rumored to be $100,000, a bargain price for a park worth at least six times that figure. In addition, the new company assumed a mortgage of $35,500 and all unpaid 1910 taxes.

The unpaid mortgage had already become a sensitive issue when Ingersoll ceased making monthly payments to the landowner in 1908. Rumors suggested that Ingersoll was planning to move the park to a new location somewhere in Cleveland, but such a plan was neither financially nor physically realistic. In desperation, the landowner sold his holdings to the Garfield Savings Bank Company, who successfully negotiated with the new Luna Park Amusement Company.

In the meantime, Ingersoll's personal situation degenerated, and in June of 1911, when a new bankruptcy case was filed, he was legally adjudged a bankrupt. Against the debt of $179,668.94 Ingersoll could declare personal assets of only three hundred dollars, including three suits of clothing. By November, Ingersoll was discharged from responsibility for all debts and claims. Although he continued to build roller coasters and other rides, Ingersoll's reputation was damaged, and his days as the owner of a string of major parks were at an end.

MR. BRAMLEY SAYS "HELLO"

With Ingersoll forever separated from Cleveland's Luna Park, majority ownership of the new Luna Park Amusement Company rested with Matthew Frederick Bramley. Although an original 1905 investor in Luna Park, Fred Bramley knew little of the daily operations of an amusement park until he acquired both Luna's assets and its liabilities. His business acumen, however, made him a splendid manager, and during the next decade the Luna Park Amusement Company generated outstanding profits. In some years, shareholders enjoyed dividends as high as 125 percent per share.

Bramley was born in 1868 at Independence, Ohio. His parents were English immigrants who operated a farm where Fred worked long hours while attending school. After hauling ice to breweries for a time, Bramley drove teams of horses for a Cleveland paving contractor and then spent several years working in a bank. During the 1890s, he founded the Cleveland Trinidad Paving Company. Soon this company was the largest paving concern in the world and maintained offices in Cleveland, New York, Columbus, and Detroit. Among the firm's projects was the paving of New York's famous Fifth Avenue. As the demand for paved streets grew, so did Fred Bramley's fortunes and soon he was a millionaire.

Once he was financially secure, Bramley pursued other interests. A life-long devotion to the Republican Party did not prevent him from becoming a close friend of Tom L. Johnson, Cleveland's Democratic reform mayor. Bramley served in the State House of Representatives in 1898 and was a key member of the City Hall Commission for more than a decade. Prominent in Cleveland's construction industry, his appointment to the Building Commission in 1905 probably came as a surprise to no one.

Bramley was more than a wealthy businessman who dabbled in politics. He was an early environmentalist and a proponent of reforestation. He spent large sums of money developing lakes and planting trees on the more than eight thousand acres he owned in and around Cleveland. Some of these parcels were devoted to agricultural enterprises, and Bramley owned more than fifty farms that raised Hereford and Black Angus cattle. It may have been because of his many and varied interests that Bramley became captivated with Luna Park.

During the 1911 season, Bramley decided to serve as the park's manager. Considering his numerous business and civic commitments, however, it is not surprising that he soon found himself overwhelmed by the daily attention that a large amusement park required. A year later he replaced himself as manager with Charles X. Zimerman. Even tempered, disciplined, and the master of any situation, Zimerman knew little about amusement parks. In fact, Zimerman freely admitted that when he entered the gates of Luna he was paying his first visit to an amusement park. Fortunately, Zimerman was a highly qualified manager who learned the business quickly.

Born in Cleveland in 1865, Zimerman spent a number of years as a bookkeeper before being appointed assistant auditor of the City of Cleveland in 1910. He was best known, however, for his long and successful military career. In 1884, Zimerman enlisted as a private in the 5th Infantry Regiment, Ohio National Guard. Three years later he was commissioned a lieutenant, and he left Cleveland for Spanish-American War service as a captain and company commander. Soon after his return from the southern camps, he was promoted to colonel and assumed command of the 5th Regiment. Because Zimerman was one of the area's best known citizen-soldiers, he was always addressed as "colonel."

Colonel (later General) Charles X. Zimerman, Luna's capable and respected park manager.
Cleveland *Press* Collection, Cleveland State University

THE LUNA NEIGHBORHOOD – A CULTURAL MIX

While Luna Park was undergoing sweeping changes in management, the community surrounding the park was experiencing its own evolution. Originally, the area around the park was an ethnic mix and included a large number of Hungarian families living near Woodland Avenue. This began to change in 1910 when the Sebatta family moved to East 110th and Ingersoll Road, directly across from the park's northeast corner. Within a year, the Sebattas were joined by the families of Luigi Mancini, Gennaro Olivo, and Frank Timperio. Other Italian families soon

A typical bungalow on one of the streets that surrounded Luna Park. On summer evenings, the residents enjoyed an unsurpassed view of the park's lights from the second floor porch.

Author's Collection

followed, and the outskirts of the park became Cleveland's third major Italian community on the East Side. The oldest community, Big Italy, was located on Woodland Avenue from Ontario and Orange Avenues to East 40th Street. Little Italy was located on Murray Hill from East 119th to East 125th Streets.

Those who settled around the park after 1910 were primarily from Compobasso in the south central portion of Italy and from the town of Rionero Sannitico. By 1920, there were 653 Italian families settled around Luna Park; and by 1930 the number reached 1,233 households.

As might be expected, Luna's employees increasingly came from the Italian families in the area. Soon, entire families worked at the park. And, those who did not work at the park found entertainment there. In response to the growing Italian patronage, Bramley and Zimerman began to engage Italian concert bands. Three local bands, Gugliotta's, Frank Russo's, and Dominic Villoni's, were enthusiastically supported by the Italian community. Naturally, these bands spent many summer afternoons and evenings at the park's Concert Garden. When the Banda Rosa, Italy's finest municipal band, toured the United States, it was booked for a full two weeks at Luna. Eugenio Sorrentino, the band's dashing, wavy-haired and mustachioed leader, was understandably a big hit with Luna's Italian neighbors. Gradually, a bond was formed between Luna Park and Cleveland's newest Italian neighborhood – a mutually beneficial friendship that lasted until the park closed.

A NEW REGIME – NEW ATTRACTIONS

The Bramley-Zimerman regime brought many positive changes to Luna Park. Old attractions, many no longer very popular, were removed. Obsolete rides were replaced with the newest in mechanical thrillers. Buildings that were no longer functional were razed. At the same time, however, both men realized that much of Ingersoll's formula for a successful amusement park was as sound in 1915 as it had been in 1905. Ingersoll's best ideas remained, while others were improved and expanded.

Due to the small acreage of Luna Park, efficient utilization of space was essential.

Author's Collection

The big competitor for both vaudeville and the circus acts was the moving picture. By 1916, movies were exhibited at 170 locations around Cleveland, and local theaters claimed a total of 85,000 seats. Daily attendance at these theaters averaged more than one hundred thousand and that number tripled on Sundays. Movies were drawing people away from amusement parks, so the parks countered by offering their own movies. Luna started exhibiting free movies every evening in the German Village; and advertising highlighted the fact that for ten cents visitors to Luna received not only free movies, but also three daily vaudeville shows, two band concerts, and a balloon ascension. Here was a non-stop entertainment bill that no movie theatre could match.

In addition to the free showing of movies, Luna also used movies as the basis for promotions. When the Moving Picture Exhibitors' League held an outing at the park in 1912, the public was invited to have their "picture taken" on moving picture film. And, as Charlie Chaplin's popularity crested, Luna created Charlie Chaplin Nights. Every Tuesday night during 1915, anyone who dressed like Chaplin was admitted to the park free. This offer generally attracted fifty "Chaplins" a week, some looking remarkably like the movie star (one particularly convincing Chaplin impersonator was Bob Hope). Once inside, the imitators were encouraged to perform Chaplin routines, and prizes ranging from two to ten dollars were awarded to the best impersonators. As this promotion developed over the summer, large crowds started appearing to watch the Chaplinesque antics.

On With the Dance

Ingersoll's original plans for Luna Park included a cavernous dance pavilion located next to the Japanese exhibit, a few yards from the end of the Shoot-the-Chutes lagoon. Although dancing was a popular pastime, ballrooms often were considered unsavory places. Many served as haunts for prostitutes, and the numerous hard-drinking male patrons. Urban dance halls deserved the reputation they acquired, but properly policed ballrooms, like those at Cedar Point, Euclid Beach, and Luna Park, often suffered from an association with their less respectable competitors.

By 1910, civic-minded Clevelanders tired of the disgraceful conduct that occurred in local ballrooms and formed the unofficial Public Dance Hall Commission. The commission investigated the city's 130 dance halls, and their reports stirred so much moral indignation that city council passed an ordinance providing for the inspection and regulation of dance halls. The mayor promptly appointed a dance hall inspector, forty male deputies, and two female chaperones to handle more delicate situations that involved ladies.

Colonel Zimerman and his staff, who already ran a well supervised dance floor, cooperated fully with the city. Rules were strict: if a man rolled up his sleeves or wore a soft collar, he was asked to leave. Girls whose dance styles offended even the " . . . more moderate Tango people," were also escorted to the door. Of course, drunken behavior or improper body contact during a dance immediately attracted both the city dance inspectors and Luna's dance hall staff.

Although more tolerant than Euclid Beach, Luna still earned a sterling reputation. According to a recreation survey conducted at the time of World War I, "No dance floor in the city is more free from objectionable features." In addition to inspectors and chaperons, policemen and floor managers were always highly visible. "A high standard of decorum," reported the survey," is maintained both on the floor and on the platform. On the whole, the management of Luna Park deserves high praise for the standard which it has set."

By the time the 1914 season opened, some dance floor rules were becoming difficult to enforce. Around that time, Irene and Vernon Castle introduced a variety of new "society dances." While the Castles helped to legitimize the ballroom, not every dance hall operator approved of the new dances. The new steps, including the Castle Walk, the Media Luna, Innovation, Hesitation, the Skating Step, the Lame Duck, and the Side Waltz, were promptly banned at the conservative Euclid Beach. Luna, always more tolerant than Euclid Beach, welcomed the new steps, and by June the Tango, the High Jinks, the One Step, and a dozen other contemporary dances debuted.

Park photographer Bert Chatfield, with the oriental tower of Luna's new ballroom in the background.

Frances Davenport Collection

Ballroom managers who permitted the new dances assumed that they would mean greater profits. However, some doubt must have entered their minds when Cedar Point president George Boeckling banned the Tango at that resort on July 22, 1914. It was not that Boeckling felt the Tango was immoral. Rather, dance hall revenues had fallen by two thousand dollars since the introduction of the new dances. It seems that the new dances required both practice and talent. As a result, more people watched and fewer bought dance tickets. Luna maintained its policy regarding modern dances for awhile, but by 1918 many of the new dances were banned and the dance hall reverted to a more sedate pace.

Regardless of the controversies over dance hall regulations and the new dance steps, ballroom dancing became big business at Luna Park. Soon, the original 1905 dance hall was no longer adequate, and in 1917, Bramley spent $100,000 to construct a new ballroom on the site of the original building. At a time when any dance hall with more than 5,000 square feet was considered a large hall, Luna's new facility had 18,000 square feet of dance floor.

The era of romantic dancing had arrived at Luna. "The floor is perfect," noted one newspaper reporter, "the music-shall we say adorable?" Even though the new ballroom was carefully policed and inspected, it was still the perfect retreat for young couples. "They dance and dance, and visit the soda grill above, and dance again." Interestingly, the reporter noted that there were thousands of couples who visited the dance hall regularly but never saw other parts of the park. As far as the park's other attractions were concerned, "They hardly know there are others."

Each three minute dance in Luna's ballroom cost five cents. The nickel dance prevailed at almost all Cleveland dance halls until Mayor Newton D. Baker decided that the city should enter the dance business in 1914. Two municipal dance halls were constructed, and the city offered the bargain rate of three cents per five minute dance. As he had done previously in the areas of public transportation, electricity and even ice cream in public parks, Baker exercised the city's right to compete with private business.

Even though there were larger dance halls, Cleveland's premier dance facility in 1917 was the one at Luna Park. Large enough to handle the weekend dance crowds, and comparatively relaxed when compared with strict Euclid Beach, the dance hall promptly became one of Luna's key attractions. As one observer reported, "...there are many nights when its turnstiles cannot click fast enough to suit the crowds which throng about it." In the years that followed, dancing would attain a new level of importance at Luna and throughout the amusement world.

The pool was opened with much ceremony. On the first day, the Cleveland Swimming Club held races, and Guy Dailey, the Human Fish, was engaged to give underwater swimming exhibitions. According to Colonel Zimerman, who used his pocket watch to time the swimmer, Dailey could remain underwater for a full four minutes. Dailey also gave swimming lessons for women and children, and the park made sure that the pool catered to the fairer sex. The pool was reserved exclusively for ladies between 9:00 a.m. and noon every day. In addition, they assured the women of Cleveland that Luna protected them from the embarrassments of the public beaches. "Ladies and children can swim here without fear of being offended by the host of smart alecks one finds at the public bathing places. Luna will not tolerate either offensive actions or conversation on the part of anyone visiting the lake." Appreciative daily crowds of up to three thousand took advantage of Luna's outstanding swimming facility.

Just as the 1915 season was about to start, Colonel Zimerman addressed the propriety of ladies' bathing attire. Annette Kellermann, a shapely actress, swimmer, and diver, had recently introduced a one-piece bathing suit at Revere Beach near Boston. She was promptly arrested, but the Kellermann bathing suit was gaining in popularity across the country. Fearing the appearance of one-piece suits at Luna, Zimerman announced that the Kellermann suit would not be allowed at Lake Luna. But the ladies of Cleveland were anxious to embrace the new

style. Mrs. S. H. Schmidt designed a one-piece suit that was similar to Annette's but, "does not show off one's figure…." The colonel approved the new suit design, and by early June several dozen daring ladies wearing new swim attire graced Lake Luna.

The controversy over the Kellermann fashion soon faded, but Zimerman noticed that the publicity attracted people to the pool, especially young men! Before the 1916 season opened, Zimerman recruited a corps of a dozen attractive models to adorn the beach. The colonel admitted that they were selected, "…for their swimming ability as well as for looks and good figures." The models were paid for "swimming, diving and floating," but actually their main function was to attract attention to the pool. It was hoped that the better swimmers would eventually become lifeguards or teach shy ladies to swim, but it was clear that Luna's management had learned that not everyone came to the beach to swim.

MINDING THE MIDWAY

Although hundreds of thousands of dollars were spent on the ballroom, the skating rink, and the pool, Bramley never forgot that Luna was, first and foremost, an amusement park. As such, mechanical rides were the primary attraction, but many of the rides installed in 1905 were

Bramley's answer to Euclid Beach's sandy bathing area was Lake Luna, which opened in 1914.
Author's Collection

From high atop the Shoot-the-Chutes, the vista displays the lagoon, the entrance gate, and the city beyond.
Norman Petri Collection, Courtesy of Lee O. Bush

becoming obsolete. New rides were coming on the market every year, and each season larger and faster roller coasters were constructed. In 1913, Euclid Beach contracted with Ingersoll and his designer, John Miller, for the construction of a great racing coaster, the Derby Racer. Suddenly, Luna's Scenic Railway and Figure Eight coaster seemed antiquated. In addition, Euclid Beach installed an elaborate Philadelphia Toboggan Company carousel in 1910. Luna's original carousel, although attractive, could not match the grandeur of the new Euclid Beach machine. Knowing that new rides were necessary if Luna was to remain Cleveland's favorite park, Bramley launched an expensive campaign to install new rides in 1914.

The budget for improvements in 1915 was set at $160,000, included provisions for an ornate carousel costing $18,000 and a modern, high speed roller coaster priced at $25,000. In the late fall of 1914, Bramley had met with Henry Auchy, president of the Philadelphia

Toboggan Company, and signed an agreement for the construction of both rides. Before Christmas, Philadelphia Toboggan carvers were busy carving horses, and Joe McKee had completed plans for the new coaster. It was a busy winter at Philadelphia Toboggan. In 1915, the company installed six large carousels and four roller coasters around the country. Interestingly, one of the coasters was designed for Luna's rival, Willoughbeach Park.

Luna's new carousel was delivered and in place by May 10, 1915. Typical of the Philadelphia Toboggan machines, it was a beautifully ornate carousel with sixty-eight horses arranged in four rows. In addition, there were two exquisitely carved Roman-style chariots. One was adorned with a large eagle, the other with a lion that held a shield with the maker's "PTC" initials clearly visible. The upper edges of the chariots were studded with large colorful gems. When operating at full capacity, the new carousel could carry more than one thousand riders per hour. Music for the carousel was provided by a large band organ built by the French firm of Gavioli & Company and imported by New York's Berni Organ Company. Capable of duplicating a band or orchestra of about forty-five pieces, the carousel's organ could be heard in every corner of the park.

Although the carousel was ready to operate long before opening day, finishing the new Jack Rabbit coaster was a more difficult task. Before the new coaster could be constructed, the old Figure Eight coaster had to be removed. Its structure, cars, machinery, and motor were offered for sale, but by February there were still no buyers. As a result, construction of the Jack Rabbit was delayed until March. Beginning May 1, crews worked day and night to complete the ride, and on the day before opening Colonel Zimerman took the first ride on the new coaster. Advertised as "The King Speedway of America," the Jack Rabbit was a medium-size coaster with moderate hills and speed. In keeping with Luna's architecture, the facade of its loading station featured a stylized pagoda.

During the winter of 1916, the Philadelphia Toboggan Company was engaged by Luna once more. This time Gus Weiss, the company's carousel horse artist, painted, varnished, and stenciled Luna's eight Shoot-the-Chutes boats. The total cost was thirty-two dollars for labor and twenty dollars for paint!

In 1916, Bramley again invested a great deal of money in midway improvements. Most of the budget was spent on an imposing Ferris Wheel erected not far from the carousel building

This magnificent carousel, built by the Philadelphia Toboggan Company, was part of Bramley's 1915 improvement program.
Frederick Fried Archives

New for 1916, the large Ferris Wheel situated near the carousel building.
Author's Collection

Designed by Walter P. Shaw and built by his Coney Island firm, the Park Construction Company, the new wheel towered 123 feet above the concrete midway. Luna's advertising claimed it was the largest Ferris Wheel in the United States and at that time, it may have been. The wheel supported twelve enclosed cars, each capable of seating a dozen or more people. At night, Luna's illuminated wheel could be seen far and wide. A similar Shaw wheel owned by Colonel Zimerman was installed at Akron's Summit Beach Park when that facility opened in 1917.

Many smaller rides, including The Whip, which was introduced to Luna's patrons in 1918, were also added. One rider recalled The Whip as a ride "admirably calculated to jerk lose one's worries and send them flying." However, Luna

"THE WHIP"

The Whip was purchased in 1918, and the ride's inventor, William Mangels, was so proud of the installation that he included this photo in his company's catalog.
Courtesy of Vestal Press, Ltd.

small stick pin. In addition, he claimed that the park employed shills to entice the unwary to games where they lost money without any rewards. The park's spokesman, J. H. Ludwig, expressed surprise at the charges and indicated that the games had operated since 1905 without any complaints. In any case, Ludwig reminded the public, only the motordrome, the swimming pool, and the baseball diamond were in the City of Cleveland. The rest of the park, including all games, were situated in Newburgh and beyond Cleveland's legal jurisdiction.

The Gregg controversy died as quickly as it had materialized, but it seems that Luna always incited controversy. It was not that the management of Luna was permissive. They strictly adhered to city dance hall rules and prohibited holding hands in the darkened caverns of the Mystic River ride and on the midway. Public displays of affection and drunken behavior were never permitted by Bramley or the straight-laced Zimerman. Still, the park was forever the target of reformers, and the slightest infraction aroused the pious. In 1915, a Cleveland lady brought legal action against the park for a personal injury. Such cases were common in the amusement park industry and generally attracted little interest or attention. However, in this case the prosecutor learned that one of jurors and a friend had visited the park and received all of the complimentary ride and attraction tickets they could use. As proof, the juror handed the prosecutor $1.40 worth of unused tickets. The park's management could never be tied to this embarrassment and, in fact, the final verdict stated that management had not been involved. Nevertheless, the impropriety was never fully explained.

GOOD COMPANY AND FAMILY GATHERINGS

Throughout the park's history, organized picnics were the life blood of Luna. The park staff spent the entire winter booking picnics and enticing groups away from Euclid Beach and Willoughbeach Park. Some picnics had been at Luna almost from the day the park opened. The butchers' picnic was heralded as the largest amusement park picnic in the United States. In 1912, the butchers served three thousand pounds of roast beef on fifteen hundred loaves of bread. Two years later, they proudly announced that 100,000 roast beef sandwiches were consumed by picnickers. The Municipal Market Men's picnic of 1914 was another enormous event. It drew twenty-eight thousand guests in the afternoon and another fifteen thousand by evening. The major attraction was a prize drawing with a five-passenger automobile as the grand prize. Other prizes included 5,680 peck baskets filled with 48,000 pounds of bread, coffee, cheese, soap, potatoes, and other commodities.

The picnic groups that selected Luna for their summer outings were as numerous as they were diverse. Among the major events were the annual Labor Day picnics of the American Federation of Labor that brought fifty thousand to the park for the conclusion of the summer season. In addition, there was Equal Suffrage Day, Newburgh Day, the International Typographers' Union picnic, and when a state encampment was held in Cleveland in 1911, a Grand Army of the Republic Day, complete with Civil War drills and demonstrations. Imancipation Day continued until after the First World War, but blacks were becoming increasingly unhappy with their treatment by both the park and the city. Although the mayor of Cleveland attended many events at the park, the vice mayor generally represented the city on Emancipation Day.

A new annual event, conceived by Colonel Zimerman and concessionaire Charles Salen, began with the first Children's Day on July 1, 1915. On that day, twenty-five thousand "deserving

Free passes to Luna Park were highly coveted. Most, however, were reserved for politicians, the, press, and special friends of management.
Author's Collection

The park's skyline as seen from Woodhill Road.   Cleveland Public Library

What's an outing without a formal picture? (circa 1916)
Richard F. Hershey Collection

In command of Luna's police force was Chief Fred W. Scheutzow. Because of the parks large crowds and free-flowing beer, Scheutzow and his men were kept busy.

Eleanor D. Loede Collection

children of the city" were treated to free admission and rides. The event was soon managed by a large committee of Clevelanders and food donations were solicited from the city's merchants months before the event. In 1916, a partial list of donations included six hundred pounds of ham, twelve thousand loaves of bread, a half-ton of candy, and hundreds of gallons of ice cream. Tickets were distributed freely at schools, social centers and settlement houses. Of course, no event this large could escape certain problems. The 1916 Children's Day was something of a nightmare for park police as well as

Luna's miniature steam train was a favorite with the children.
Western Reserve Historical Society

the office staff. Over the course of the day, more than 300 lost children were escorted to the park office. As closing time neared, one unclaimed child remained and Salen, whose wife was also an organizer of the event, took the child home until the parents could be located the next day.

No matter how crowded and noisy the midway may have been, everyone was kept well informed of the day's happenings by Luna's king of ballyhoo, John "Moxie" Cross. Moxie spent his winters with indoor circuses and his summers at Luna. Equipped only with a megaphone, his daily duties included announcing schedule changes and special events from noon until midnight. Always nattily attired in a business suit, Moxie could be heard throughout the park. On a clear day, it was said, his voice could be heard two miles from the park! Moxie Cross was one of Luna's most memorable characters.

On days when picnics were not scheduled, Colonel Zimerman devised special events to attract park visitors. When conventions were in Cleveland, heavy advertising enticed out-of-towners to a park that promised to be the best equipped amusement park west of New York. At the end of the season was a Harvest Festival that promised dancing, food, beverages, and prizes. Late in the 1913 season, management began a search for a couple that would agree to be married on the park's big Concert Garden stage. James Smith, the park's own chief of police, and his fiancee, Stella Jepson, volunteered. In return for using the couple as a promotional gimmick,

the park paid all wedding expenses, gave the bride a new piano, and provided Smith with boxes of cigars and bottles of wine.

The most bizarre event to take place at Luna came in 1915 when a Cleveland physician, Jean Dawson, launched an anti-fly campaign. Understanding that flies could carry disease, children were encouraged to collect and kill flies. One boy reported killing six thousand flies before the summer was half over! Luna participated in the crusade by offering season passes to the one hundred children who killed the most flies. In addition, the winners spent a full day at the park with all rides and attractions provided without charge. Whether or not the children were required to present boxes of dead flies to verify their claims was never discussed.

THE WARTIME ECONOMY

America's entry into the World War in April of 1917 began an era of change and uncertainty for Luna and hundreds of other amusement parks. Ironically, in August of 1914, Luna started posting daily war bulletins in the German Village! World events actually began to affect Luna in June of 1916 when the 5th Infantry was mobilized for service on the Mexican border. Among the fifteen hundred National Guardsmen to leave were regimental commander Zimerman, and a number of other park employees. Zimerman and the 5th Regiment were not back in Cleveland very long when they learned in May of 1917 that they would be going to France as a unit of the new 37th Division. By July, the regiment had departed for camp and Luna was left without its able manager. However, Zimerman enjoyed a distinguished wartime career. He was commissioned a brigadier general and went to France in command of the 73rd Infantry Brigade, serving in the Baccarat Sector and in the Meuse-Argonne Offensive. In September of 1918, General Zimerman was injured when thrown from a horse and was sent back to the United States where he was discharged in February, 1919.

By the time Zimerman was leaving for camp, the draft had been established and the military was siphoning off park employees and patrons alike. The park did its part to support the war effort, and on Sunday, June 24, 1917, the

Just before the United States entered the First World War, the Ohio National Guard's 5th Regiment Band performed at Luna. Many of the bandsmen were also members of Gugliotta's Band.

Dominic Gugliotta Collection

park's entire gate receipts (about two thousand dollars) were donated to the Red Cross Fund. They also staged a gigantic military firework display called "Wake Up America" at the baseball grounds. Tickets were available for fifty cents, seventy-five cents, or one dollar, and a major portion of the ticket sales was donated to the Recruiting Fund.

The war brought certain changes to the park. Keen observers noted that the shooting gallery was busier than usual. Mustachioed men with foreign accents, boys who expected to be in the trenches within months, and even some girls crowded around the gallery. Said one newspaper reporter, "They forget the difference between a 22-caliber Winchester and a high power military rifle. A nation unaccustomed to arms is interested in the business before it, and there must be a measure of education in shooting even at bells and tin rabbits and geese."

The food concessionaires, too, observed changes. There was talk of a sugar shortage and the possibility that the government would purchase the entire 1917 wheat crop. Many amusement park foods and beverages required sugar, and wheat was a major ingredient of hot dog buns and waffles. The shortages did not materialize, but wholesale food prices did rise as the war progressed. When the 1917 season started, Weiss sold chicken dinners in the park restaurant for seventy-five cents. In June of 1918 the price reached $1.25 and by August, $1.50. Almost as an apology for escalating prices they were advertised as the "best chicken dinners in the city."

Luna adjusted well to the wartime economy, the rising cost of supplies, the shortage of young male employees, and the public's increasing need for diversions from the concerns of war. It was during the war that the park first offered a fifty-cent combination ticket that bought admission to the park and a dollar's worth of midway attractions. If money became scarce, the combination ticket was designed to be perceived as an unequalled bargain. Most parks, in fact, did very well during the 1917 and 1918 seasons. However, one of Luna's longtime competitors, Silver Lake Park near Cuyahoga Falls, failed to open in 1918. Once a strong amusement park that surprising numbers of Clevelanders reached by

interurban cars, Silver Lake was demolished and converted into a restricted residential development. Bay Park, a short-lived competitor located on the lake, never caught the public's interest and closed a number of years before the war. Gradually, the Cleveland amusement park market was becoming a battleground for two: Luna, advertised as "Cleveland's Only Amusement Park," and, on the outskirts of the city, Euclid Beach.

ROARING TOWARD THE TWENTIES

Between 1910 and 1918, Luna Park was at its zenith. During these years it was Cleveland's premier amusement park and all others fought for second place. The park's architecture, its continuous bill of entertainment, the free flowing beer, and maybe even a feeling that at Luna there was a relaxation of morals, all contributed to the park's popularity. Also, there was Luna's nighttime illumination that, except for New York's Coney Island, was unequalled. When the Cleveland Recreation Survey was conducted immediately after the First World War, a young lady who worked in a garment factory and who was a regular customer at Luna was taken for the first time to Euclid Beach. After only a few minutes she commented, "Why don't they have more lights here? Gee! this place is dead." Luna's overwhelming display of incandescent lamps was possibly its most memorable feature.

The nightly illumination of Luna was visible for miles.
Cleveland Public Library

ON WITH THE SHOW

The attendance figures released by amusement park press agents were often grossly inflated. Small parks, whose facilities would be taxed by a crowd of 15,000, sometimes claimed crowds of 60,000 or even 100,000. Certainly some of the numbers that Luna's staff provided for newspaper stories were exaggerations, but much evidence suggests that attendance at Luna before 1920 was impressive. On opening day of 1914 and again on Labor Day of 1916, fifty thousand park visitors were counted. The entire 1916 season, according to Colonel Zimerman, drew 1,967,435 people. During the first six weeks of the 1917 season, attendance stood at 627,286 and concessionaires reported a twenty-five percent increase in business. Unsure of the meaning of this increase, Zimerman theorized that either people had more money in their pockets or, because of war worries, had more need for recreation. While these attendance figures may have been subject to some manipulation by the park manager, later research conducted for the Cleveland Recreation Survey suggests that they were fairly honest and accurate.

Luna had already been closed for several months when the war ended in France. No one at Luna or any other amusement park could have even dreamed that the post war world would be so different from what they had known before 1917. Unknown to everyone, Luna Park's reign as the queen of Northern Ohio's amusement parks was at an end. New laws, social trends, and economic patterns ushered in Luna's final era. Never again would the park attain the stature that it had enjoyed in 1915.

A trio of young men in Chatfield's photo studio.
Courtesy of Mary Clare Yarham

For those who wanted a photo souvenir with a pleasant background, Bert Chatfield offered a number of painted canvas scenes.   Frances Davenport Collection

(left) Bert Chatfield, owner of Luna's photo studio, poses in front of his own camera.
Frances Davenport Collection

Photo studio patrons who desired a more dignified photograph could pose in Chatfield's open touring car.
Author's Collection

The bridge that spanned the Shoot-the-Chutes lagoon was a popular place for snapshots.
Frances Davenport Collection

Two of the more than one million people who visited Luna each season relax behind the Figure Eight roller coaster.
Author's Collection

CHAPTER FIVE
THE UNEVEN

PROSPERITY OF THE 1920s

The summer that followed the end of the First World War was a period of uncertainty in the amusement park industry. Although the armistice had occurred six months earlier, Germany had not agreed to treaty terms. There was a possibility that the Allied armies might still be required to invade the defeated nation. Considering this, and the fact that many wartime government controls remained in effect, park owners were cautious and invested little in improvements.

The exotic, colorful entrance gate that greeted visitors was fitted with hundreds of incandescent lights.
Ohio Historical Society

Coney Island, at the forefront of the industry since the 1890s, best reflected the mood of 1919. Karl Kitchen, a New York reporter, visited Coney early in the season and related that the resort had not changed very much since 1918. There were no new rides or attractions, except for some new murderers in the Eden Musee wax museum. Worse, prices had increased alarmingly. Sightseeing cars raised their rates from fifty cents to one dollar. The five cent beer was being replaced by the fifteen cent "near beer," and the nickel hot dog was now fifteen cents at many stands. A modest dinner, which might have cost $1.50 before the war, was now $4.00. Postwar inflation was as obvious on the midway as it was in the department store and the grocery store.

Another indicator of industry uncertainty was a general sluggishness in amusement ride sales and construction. The Philadelphia Toboggan Company, a major park outfitter, built only three roller coasters in 1919, compared to eleven in 1926, and nine in 1927. Similarly, they delivered only three carousels, compared to six in 1915 and the same number in 1920. Overall, the industry did not yet have any reason to assume that the 1920s would be prosperous.

...AND NOT A DROP TO DRINK

For Luna Park and the hundreds of other parks that sold beer and derived a huge portion of their annual profits from alcoholic beverages, the certainty of prohibition loomed more ominously than economic uncertainty. The Eighteenth Amendment had already been ratified, assuring that prohibition would be the law of the land by 1920. However, on November 21, 1918, the War Prohibition Act was passed. This act made the sale of intoxicating beverages illegal after June 30, 1919, and until such time as President Wilson proclaimed an end to the war and demobilization period. At Luna, plans to continue selling beer until June 30 evaporated when Ohio was voted dry before either of the national prohibition laws could take effect.

On Saturday, May 24, Cleveland's nine breweries made their last deliveries. Two days later the city's thirteen hundred saloons closed. The impact of prohibition on both Cleveland and Luna Park cannot be overstated. Cleveland's brewing industry produced nine million dollars worth of beer annually and the largest brewery alone sold 500,000 barrels. At Leisy's Brewery,

where almost 400,000 barrels were filled a year, Otto Leisy estimated that prohibition would put 1,800 Cleveland brewery employees out of work. Suddenly, long-popular brands of beer disappeared, including The Pilsener Brewing Company's beloved P.O.C. (Pilsener of Cleveland). Leisy's, like many other breweries, adjusted as best it could by switching production to carbonated soft drinks. Soon, Leisy's ginger ale, root beer, loganberry, and orangeade replaced beer on the delivery trucks. At Luna, the transition to a dry environment was equally painful.

Economic uncertainty and the end of beer sales were serious concerns for Bramley and his manager, William Reutener. But these concerns were quickly overshadowed when the Red Scare surfaced violently in Cleveland on May 1. Not unexpectedly, a Socialist parade was approached by a group of patriotic Victory Loan workers who requested that the red flags be lowered. The Cleveland Police entered the fray and soon anti-socialist riots spread throughout the city. Before the day was over, there were two deaths, scores were injured, and the Socialist headquarters was destroyed. With similar violence taking place around the country, Bramley and Reutener had good reason to fear that anti-red disturbances would spread to amusement parks during the coming hot summer months. The gates to Luna opened on schedule, but management remained tense, and uniformed security officers were more numerous than ever.

LUNA PERSISTS IN THE MARKETPLACE

That spring, advertisements for Luna proclaimed "100 New Features," but visitors would be hard-pressed to locate even one significant improvement. In fact, very little had been spent on the park due to the recent end of the war and the economy. The only noticeable addition was a restaurant that specialized in chicken and steak dinners and adopted the slogan "famous for clean food." The new facility featured entertainment during the dinner hours and late into the evening. The American Harmony Four, a quartet that sang " ... negro melodies, the latest in comic opera and the season's vaudeville hits," was typical of the entertainment offered by the restaurant. The shows for the restaurant, as well as all of the acts that performed throughout the park, were under contract with Fred Brandt, Luna's newly appointed booking manager. For the next several years, Brandt worked to modernize the park's live shows and free acts. Vaudeville was quickly dying, and numerous vaudeville theaters had already been converted to movie theaters. As a result, acts that were "at liberty" were plentiful in 1919.

Since the day it opened, Luna had always utilized slogans in newspaper advertising. "Cleveland's Fairyland of Pleasure" was probably the most consistently used slogan in the years before the World War. After the war, management seems to have had difficulty finding an appropriate slogan. In 1919, they alternated among these three rather weak phrases: "The Life Giving Park; The Happyland Park; Gloom Gives Way to Joy at Luna." Management's inability to settle on one descriptive slogan for the 1919 season is indicative of the uncertainty that plagued them throughout the season.

If anything restored confidence at Luna, it was the strong organized picnic business that was, except during the economically depressed 1921 season, a hallmark of the era. Transportation had not yet returned to a normal peacetime mode, and many groups that traditionally planned their picnics at distant parks like Cedar Point or Buckeye Lake, stayed near home. Among these groups was the annual Newburgh Merchants outing that was normally held outside

As suggested in this photo of Cleveland streetcar advertising, Luna's management began placing more emphasis on the park's restaurant during the 1920s.
Courtesy of Norman Buckholtz

The Six Flying La Vans
appeared at Luna in 1919.
Circus World Museum,
Baraboo, Wisconsin

-100-

Another circus star to perform at Luna in 1919 was high wire artist Berta Beeson.

Circus World Museum, Baraboo, Wisconsin

of the Cleveland area. In 1919, however, the event's frustrated committee could not arrange for adequate railroad service and so selected Luna for the August event. For Luna, it was a major triumph. On Newburgh Merchants' Day even the city's big steel plants were closed so that workers could attend the picnic with their families.

The war was responsible for the founding of some new veterans' groups that held their first amusement park picnics in 1919. The American Legion came to Luna late in the 1919 season for the first of many picnics. This Legion picnic was particularly meaningful, for General C. R. Edwards was sent to the park to decorate a number of the Cleveland's war heroes.

In a season of social and economic upheaval, Luna's management took some extraordinary steps to attract larger crowds. One of these steps was to sign a contract with Sells-Floto Circus to bring the big tent show to Luna in late July. Tickets went on sale at the park and at downtown stores weeks before the show. On July 27, the circus pitched its tents just outside Luna's fence. Curious Clevelanders were encouraged to visit the menagerie tent, the horse tent, and the cook tent, while performers on the back lot did their laundry and rehearsed their acts. On the following day, a generally quiet Monday in the park business, a circus parade left Luna and wound through the nearby streets. Performances were held twice during the afternoon, and by sunset the Sells-Floto Circus was striking its tents for the move to the next engagement.

Park manager Reutener announced that Luna would close on the Sunday following Labor Day, but noted that the park would be available throughout September for groups looking for a place to hold traditional clambakes. However, the attempt to schedule post-season events was not successful and was seldom repeated.

When the gates closed for the season, a relieved Reutener announced that, "The management thanks its many patrons for their support during the season of 1919." While the 1919 season was far better than had been anticipated, it could not touch those flush years before the war. Due in large part to the cessation of beer sales at Luna, attendance began to drop sharply in 1919. For the first time since the park opened in 1905, its seasonal attendance fell below that of Euclid Beach. Unaffected by a ban on alcohol

When Zimerman returned to Cleveland in 1919, Bramley apparently felt an obligation to retain Reutener as park manager while making Zimerman president of the Trinidad Paving Company. Reutener seems to have been a competent manager, but he had the misfortune to assume control of Luna at the time when the park lost beer sales and had to confront the unfriendly economy of 1921. After the financial disaster of the 1921 season, Reutener was replaced as park manager by Zimerman. At about the same time, Zimerman was elected mayor of Euclid, and he served in that office until 1925. Whether the promotional and organizational expertise of Zimerman would erase the park's post-war problems remained to be seen.

General Zimerman wasted no time in reasserting his command at Luna Park. Park expansion, aggressive advertising campaigns, and effective publicity efforts proclaimed the general's return. During the next few seasons, new advertisements were created for Luna and the park placed increased orders for advertising space. The combination ticket, an experiment before the war, was installed as a regular feature. A harbinger of the pay-one-price ticket that gained favor in many parks during the 1960s and similar to a ticket plan that had been used at Coney Island's Steeplechase Park for many years, the combination ticket gave the purchaser $1.65 worth of rides and attractions for only 75 cents. However, the ticket did not cover unlimited rides, and if the visitor wanted another turn on the Jack Rabbit coaster or any of the other rides, additional tickets were required. Perhaps as a concession to the free gate policy at Euclid Beach, Zimerman also eliminated the gate charge before six p.m. every day except Sundays and holidays. Of course, complimentary passes with Zimerman's signature found their way into the hands of everyone of importance in the Cleveland area.

IN STEP, OUT OF STEP — NEW DANCE CRAZES

Although the park's dance hall did record-setting business during the 1920s, there was certainly a great deal of concern about increasing competition from new ballrooms in the Cleveland area. Immediately after the war, dance steps slowed to a shuffle, but with the Jazz Age the pace soon quickened. New dances such as the Charleston were all the rage. Suddenly, dance halls were filled to capacity and by 1924, thirty million Americans were doing the Black Bottom at least once a week.

Clevelanders greeted the new dance steps with mixed reactions. At Euclid Beach, any attempt at dancing the Charleston, especially the cheek-to-cheek version, evoked an immediate response from the dance floor supervisors. The music would stop and in a stern voice the announcer warned that Euclid Beach was not a country club and such dances were prohibited. Even if they were not doing the Charleston, couples who danced too close received a sharp rap on the shoulder. It was a different story at Luna Park. As one newspaper reporter noted," . . . you could Charleston until your legs dropped off and no one cared." Despite Luna's more relaxed atmosphere, Euclid Beach's ballroom sold more tickets. During a typical week, Euclid Beach sold seventy-six thousand dance tickets to Luna's forty-four thousand.

When it came to ballrooms, however, Euclid Beach was not Luna's primary competition. Just after the World War there were 115 dance halls in Cleveland, as well as 8 large restaurants with

Young ladies dressed in proper flapper fashion await the release of the brakes for the next ride on the Jack Rabbit coaster.
Cleveland *Plain Dealer*

- 104 -

Dancers in Luna's ballroom were forced to observe many rules established by the city. One of the dance hall inspectors assigned to Luna park during the 1920s was Frank Menger.
Dale F. Menger Collection

The Emerson Gill Orchestra was typical of the bands that played in the ballroom of Luna park during the 1920s. Gill was most famous, however, for his engagements at the Bamboo Garden and at Chippewa Lake Park.   Author's Collection

Just as new amusement parks competed with Luna during the 1920s, so did new ballrooms. The Crystal Slipper was typical of the larger dance halls built to serve a dance-crazed public.   Author's Collection

Chippewa Lake Park added a huge new ballroom in the early 1920s and started an aggressive advertising effort in the Cleveland newspapers.
Author's Collection

licensed dance floors. Most of the dance halls were situated within a few miles of Luna's gates, but only ten of them could rival Luna in size. Probably because of the heat, many of the dance halls closed for the summer after a winter season that attracted more than one and a half million Clevelanders to their dances. However, as the 1920s progressed, not only did the number of dance halls increase, but many stayed open during the hot summer months.

A number of new dance halls opened their doors around 1924. One of the most elaborate was Euclid Gardens. Built at a cost of $500,000, Euclid Gardens opened with the Vincent Lopez.

Orchestra and quickly followed with the great Ted Weems Band. Other local halls engaged the best in local, regional, and national talent. Emerson Gill played at the Bamboo Gardens, while Austin Wylie and his ten-piece band appeared at the Golden Pheasant Restaurant on Prospect Avenue. Even dance halls outside the city solicited Cleveland business. The Moon Beach Inn in Conneaut, Ohio, advertised aggressively in Cleveland; the Lake Road Inn booked the youthful Guy Lombardo Orchestra; Akron's Summit Beach Park constructed the Wisteria Ballroom; and in Medina County, Chippewa Lake Park unveiled a cavernous new dance hall. As dancing became a national obsession, Luna's competition expanded to help meet the demand for dance facilities.

The advent of the new ballrooms brought not only competition, but also changes in admission policies. For years, both Luna Park and Euclid Beach maintained a policy that required the purchase of a ticket for each dance. If a couple intended to dance until closing time, it was best to purchase a fistful of tickets at the start of the evening. When Danceland opened at Euclid Avenue and East 90th Street in 1925, the owners initiated an admission fee of fifty cents per person. Once inside the ballroom, all dances were free. The Euclid Gardens' owners announced the same policy and so did the Crystal Slipper, although men were charged an additional twenty-five cents. How these new policies affected Luna and Euclid Beach is impossible to determine, although it is clear that dancing at one of the new ballrooms could be cheaper than attending the amusement park dance halls. Nevertheless, Luna seems to have enjoyed good patronage during most of the week. During a typical week in July or August, Luna's dance ticket sales looked like this:

Sunday	15,000
Monday	1,500
Tuesday	4,000
Wednesday	4,200
Thursday	7,000
Friday	4,000
Saturday	8,000

Bramley and Zimerman responded quickly to the new dance craze by remodelling and redecorating the ballroom in 1924 and again in 1926. With a price tag of seventy-five thousand dollars, the 1926 renovation featured an amplification system that enhanced the music in the dance hall while piping the same music into the roller skating rink.

Despite many innovations in dancing during the 1920s, Cleveland's chief dance hall inspector, Charles P. Johnson, and his one hundred inspectors steadfastly enforced some traditional 1910 regulations. Among these were rules that did not permit drinking, flirting, spooning, smoking, spitting, exaggerated or tough dancing, rowdy conduct, and the wearing of hats by men in the dance hall. In addition, prostitutes were prohibited from attending dances!

Initially, Luna Park clung to the old policy of featuring a house band exclusively throughout the season, as it did in 1923 when the Luna Jazz Band was the featured attraction. Other ballrooms, however, were booking more famous bands and drawing huge crowds. This lesson was not lost on Luna's management; soon the Luna dance hall echoed with the popular sounds of Costello's Orchestra, Charles Meade's Orchestra, Jimmie Wallace, Avellone's, and Larry Revell's Radio Revellers. The latter group broadcast dance music from Luna Park on WHK radio three nights a week.

The bands that played at Luna during the 1920s performed the popular songs of the day, including tunes like "Bye, Bye, Blackbird" and "Isn't She the Sweetest Thing." But, there was still a market for decade-old tunes and dance steps that ballroom managers called "Old Time Dances." Every Friday the bands highlighted the waltz, the schottische, and other prewar dances. In addition, special events brought ethnic music to Luna's ballroom. In 1927, the ladies of Clan Grant sponsored a Scottish night that produced some unfamiliar, but sprightly, music in the ballroom.

Despite the increasing competition from ballrooms like the Euclid Gardens, the Crystal Slipper, and Danceland, Luna's dance hall operation enjoyed excellent attendance throughout the decade. Once management realized that "name bands" drew larger crowds than the old house bands, Luna competed with the other dance halls on their level. The only competitors that Luna could not meet on even terms were the illegal speakeasies that offered dancers the added incentive of beer and liquor.

Although roller skating did not equal dancing in popularity, the roller rink was a busy place during the 1920s. The rink was renovated in 1920, enlarged in 1922, and redecorated again three seasons later. If the need for new skates is any indication of the rink's success, the operation was highly profitable. In 1924, three thousand new pairs of skates were purchased, followed by five thousand pairs in 1925 and another twelve hundred pairs in 1926. In fact, the remodeling of the rink and the buying of new skates represented a sizeable portion of the two hundred thousand dollars spent on park improvements for the 1925 season.

THE CURTAIN DESCENDS – VAUDEVILLE DECLINES

The dance hall and the skating rink were enduring success stories during the 1920s, but the decline of public interest in vaudeville shows caused management to reevaluate the park's entertainment fare. Everywhere, the public's taste in entertainment was changing and uncounted vaudeville theaters were being converted to movie houses. The massive New York Hippodrome, once the greatest variety facility in the country, closed its doors in 1923. Charles Dillingham, the building's operator since 1917, admitted that the live stage show was rapidly dying. Even though the monumental Keith's Palace Theater opened at Playhouse Square in 1922, the number of vaudeville houses in Cleveland was definitely declining. During its first year, the Palace sold almost two million tickets. But the Palace was a dinosaur almost before it opened, and in 1926 its manager began interspersing movies with the live entertainment. By 1932, movies were the Palace's primary attraction.

The immediate concern at Luna was not how to handle declining interest in vaudeville, but rather what to do with the Concert Garden where beer was dispensed during both band concerts and vaudeville shows. With beer sales now illegal, the Concert Garden sat deserted at one end of the midway. In 1920, the old Garden reopened as Russell's Famous Cabaret, with daily cabaret shows at six p.m. and ten p.m. But the cabaret was less than successful, and a year later the two-thousand-seat facility was used for a variety of outdoor shows. Typical of these shows was *A Tale of Three Cities,* a production in the old Luna tradition...offering a few snappy songs and a lot of pretty girls.

Luna stubbornly continued to offer free vaudeville, usually scheduling three daily shows. Magicians, singers, acrobats, jugglers, and dancers were still the mainstay of vaudeville, but some rather eccentric acts also appeared. Russell's Dogs was a fairly typical vaudeville canine act, but Lessik and Anita's canary and monkey act offered an unusual mix of animals.

Equally unique were some of the human performers, including Colley and Egan, who performed on the smallest piano in the world, and Suard, a master of the single string violin! One of the more sedate acts of 1921 was billed as The Act Beautiful. Similar to acts presented by some circuses at the time, the performance included a man, a woman, a horse and six setters who posed in various tableaux, including several representing fox hunting scenes. It is doubtful that The Act Beautiful kept many park visitors on the edge of their seats.

At the start of the 1922 season, General Zimerman attempted to gradually replace vaudeville with musical comedies. The new musical shows were offered four times a day and included such titles as *Stepping Lively, Charming Widows, Bell Hop's Troubles,* and *Fifteen Minutes from Broadway.* The latter was a big hit and included two black face comedians, the Six Jazz Babies, and the Metropolitan Trio (which was probably just a recycled version of the Luna Trio that appeared in an earlier show). Many of the musical shows featured at Luna from 1922 through 1925 had casts of more than fifty performers, and spotlighted what management called the "Beauty Chorus." At Luna, attractive girls were always a popular drawing card.

Zimerman's experimental musical shows met with limited success and were suspended before the end of the 1926 season. In 1927, vaudeville shows continued while the park once more tried musical comedies such as Joe Mall's *Panama Follies* and Roger Fawn's *Musical Skallywags.* A year later, both vaudeville and the musical shows were terminated.

One form of entertainment that flourished at Luna from the 1905 season until the day the park closed was the firework display. Traditionally, Luna purchased displays for July 4 and Labor Day, but often additional pyrotechnics were provided throughout the summer. And Luna's management did not skimp on their firework budgets. In 1927, they spent thirty-five hun-

dred dollars for a fabulous July 4 display. By comparison, a very good display at Orchard Lake Park on Northfield Road cost only a thousand dollars. For many years, Luna's firework exhibitions were Cleveland's best.

...BUT THE BAND PLAYED ON

Just as it had been reluctant to let go of vaudeville, Luna's management also clung steadfastly to the old fashioned band concert. During the summers of the 1920s, Sousa, Pryor, Conway, and others still toured the country and played long engagements at major amusement parks and resorts during the summer months. Starting in 1901, Sousa's Band played extended engagements at Philadelphia's Willow Grove Park each summer. These Sousa concerts were so popular that crowds often reached forty thousand. But, by 1926, people no longer came to Willow Grove for its wonderful musical offerings. Reluctantly, Sousa ended his long association with the park and moved on to Atlantic City's Steel Pier where bands were still well received. However, the decline in band concert attendance at Willow Grove Park was symptomatic of the demise of the professional concert band in America. Summer parks continued to promote band concerts, but instead of the traditional twice-a-day schedule, they were relegated to Sunday afternoons only.

Gugliotta's Band performed at Luna every season from 1905 until the park closed in 1929.
Dominic Gugliotta Collection

After the unsuccessful attempt to convert the old Concert Garden into a cabaret, it was redecorated and opened as a band concert facility in 1922. One of the musical units to play on the renamed Japanese Gardens concert stage was the Ohio National Guard's band of the 145th Infantry, directed by Lieutenant Phillip Saginor. Born in Russia, Saginor studied at the Royal Conservatory of Music and then moved to England where he was concertmaster of one of the bands of the Brigade of Guards. He arrived in Cleveland about 1914, where he served as concertmaster at the Hippodrome Theater and managed a conservatory of music. Associated with Luna Park for fifteen years, Saginor also served on the park's police force.

The other well-known band to play regularly at Luna was Gugliotta's Band, which debuted at the park in 1905. Nicola Gugliotta was one of several truly gifted Italian musicians who formed their own bands in the city's Italian neighborhoods around the turn of the century. Unlike the equally talented Frank Russo, whose band was playing over a local radio station in 1924, Gugliotta maintained a traditional concert schedule at Luna Park and Cedar Point. According to band members, Gugliotta's band was hired to play a concert for Al Capone who, it was claimed, had praised the group highly.

Gugliotta's band members were recruited almost exclusively from the director's family and from the other musical families of the east side Italian neighborhoods. Much of the music that the band played was composed by Gugliotta himself, and although he seems to have published very little, he is remembered for writing some very pleasant marches. Nick Gugliotta was not only talented but also very colorful. While visiting Canada with his band, he purchased a bear cub that he named Busy. Often, Gugliotta and Busy were seen walking in the Cleveland Metropolitan parks. Gugliotta and Luna's management must have enjoyed an excellent relationship; his band was featured at the park every season from 1905 through 1929. After Luna closed, Gugliotta moved to California where he died a few years later.

THE DIRECTION OF ENTERTAINMENT IS REROUTED

Luna's amusement park competition increased during the 1920s, primarily because of the automobile. People could now travel to other parks more easily. In addition, Euclid Beach, considered a minor facility in 1905, had blossomed into a great amusement park. Each year after 1910, the Humphrey family made major improvements at Euclid Beach. In 1921, for example, they spent $250,000 to install the Mill Chute, the largest Dodgem in the country, and the Great American Racing Derby. Over the six preceding years, they spent more than $100,000 to develop a system for mixing, carbonating, and cooling a loganberry soft drink and ginger ale. It is clear that after 1915, Luna did not keep pace with Euclid Beach's expansion programs. However, in fairness to both parks, each had its own distinctive character and each served different segments of society. Obviously, Fred Bramley and Dudley Humphrey II viewed the amusement business from very different angles.

The team of sociologists that studied both parks for the Cleveland Recreation Survey went to great lengths to compare Luna and Euclid Beach without making many qualitative judgments about either park. The most striking difference that they observed was the character of the population segment that each park served. According to the survey team, Luna was closer to the industrial center of Cleveland and as a result, appealed to more of the foreign-born citizenry. "The crowd at Luna Park is more mixed. There is a liberal proportion of markedly foreign faces, both on the dance floor and the skating rink." The rigid and puritanical standards of Euclid Beach, the researchers thought, were not appealing to the working class. The Humphrey's failure at Forest City Park, which was much closer than Euclid Beach to the working-class residential areas, was cited as proof of this theory. Working at the end of the Progressive Era, the survey writers were much impressed with Luna's ability to serve the recreational needs of the working class and felt that the American standards of recreation should be modified to better provide for the entertainment of foreign-born Americans. It is true that accents were probably more common at Luna Park, but it would be difficult to prove that Euclid Beach failed to attract large numbers from the working class. Nevertheless, the number of nationality events scheduled at each park does suggest that perhaps the ethnic communities felt more comfortable at Luna.

While Euclid Beach was perennial competition, a number of new parks flooded the area during the 1920s, although some lasted briefly. One of Cleveland's short-lived parks was Gordon Gardens which opened opposite Gordon Park at East 72nd Street on Decoration Day of 1923. The park included the Big Dipper coaster, a carousel, The Whip, an airplane swing, and a Caterpillar, all owned by Luna concessionaire Robert Loehr. Most of the food stands were owned by other Luna concessionaires, Charles Salen and Jake Mintz. A ballroom, motordrome, and bandstand completed the park's offerings. Gordon Gardens seems to have been a particularly unlucky operation. On July 22 an eighteen-year-old boy was killed when he leaned over the front seat of the Big Dipper, fell from the car, and was crushed by the speeding train. The park's economic fortunes were equally disas-

trous; the owners gladly sold the land to the City of Cleveland a few years later. Just a few miles east of Gordon Gardens, the old White City land was reactivated as a picnic area and campgrounds, serving as a camp for disabled soldiers in 1921. However, White City's hopes of competing with Luna Park had faded many years before.

Even further to the east, Mentor Beach Playland suddenly emerged with rides, dancing, bathing, an athletic field, and picnic grounds. While owners of this small park searched for group picnic bookings in Cleveland, it may have been a little too far from the city to attract any significant group business. The park survived for a number of years, but failed to make much of an impression on the Cleveland population.

A more worthy competitor was Chippewa Lake Park in Medina County, a rising star of the area's resorts. Although it had been in business since the 1870s and was served by the Cleveland Southwestern & Columbus interurban line, Chippewa Lake Park had grown slowly. In 1921, the Chippewa Lake Park Company was founded, and the new company acquired the 385 acre lake. A year later, the company was approached by Cleveland attorney Larry G. Collister, who proposed construction of an amusement midway. Collister formed the Clean Play Company and began the construction of a midway for the 1924 season. By 1927, Chippewa Lake Park was reporting gross revenues of over $170,000 and was attracting large numbers of Clevelanders to the park, the hotel, and the cottages.

The Chippewa Lake Park Company and its allied land development companies started promoting cottage communities along the eastern shore of Chippewa Lake. Lots were offered for five hundred to eleven hundred dollars, and cottages costing from five hundred to twenty thousand dollars were soon under construction. According to manager A. M. Beach, "Lots are being sold to the most desirable parties." This construction boom at Chippewa Lake was only part of a nationwide movement to establish new summer colonies along the shores of the

After an aggressive building program, Geauga Lake Park
became one of Luna's most vigorous competitors.
Bruce Young Collection

Atlantic Ocean, the Great Lakes, and on the banks of scores of smaller inland lakes. Among the many similar developments in Northern Ohio were Elberta Beach (in a peach orchard near Vermilion), Mentor Headlands, Arrowhead Beach near Willoughby, Brady Lake, Ruggles Beach, and the lovely Chaussee which stretched several miles along the Cedar Point peninsula. Like the amusement parks that often rose near these summer colonies, the summer cottage craze provided stiff competition for Luna Park. After all, city dwellers who spent their summers along the shore of a country lake had neither time nor inclination to visit inner-city Luna.

Another new park hungry for Cleveland business was Orchard Lake Park, located on Northfield Road between Hudson and Peninsula. Built and managed by Thomas E. Thorp, Orchard Lake was a forty acre site situated conveniently at stop sixty-two of the Akron, Bedford & Cleveland interurban line. The park claimed to have parking for ten thousand cars, one of the largest dance pavilions in the state, a number of amusement rides, and a natural spring lake for swimming. The park's advertising slogan, "A Refined Park for Refined People," suggests that the owners had misjudged the motivations of those attending an amusement park. Orchard Lake Park stirred a great deal of interest during its inaugural 1927 season, but it quickly faded.

Another park to fade and die during the 1920s was Willoughbeach Park. Seventeen miles from downtown Cleveland, the park was a short fifteen-minutes away thanks to the Cleveland, Painesville & Eastern traction operations. Some improvements were made to Willoughbeach in 1924, but the traction company that had owned it began to lose money the year before. The CP&E finally suspended all operations, and the last car rolled on May 20, 1926. A week later, Willoughbeach simply failed to open. As happens with most abandoned amusement parks, the rides and equipment were sold, buildings fell into disrepair, and weeds grew on the midway. Eventually, all traces of the park disappeared.

While Willoughbeach was struggling through its terminal season, the most serious threat to Luna's business emerged southeast of Cleveland. Some entertainment facilities had existed at Geauga Lake since the 1880s, but development was slow, and few people paid much attention to limited facilities on a small lake. In 1925, the small resort's anonymity ended when Geauga Lake Park was constructed. The new, modern park had parking for five thousand cars, a roller coaster that was the longest in the United States, and a swimming pool of Olympic proportions. The pool proved itself to be a particularly effective publicity tool. In 1926, future Tarzan star Johnny Weissmuller made national headlines by establishing a new world record for

the 220 yard freestyle swim at Geauga Lake. The new park was unwelcome competition for both Luna and Euclid Beach, and the fact that buses ran to the park from Cleveland for only sixty cents made Geauga Lake easily accessible. In 1927, the Erie Railroad initiated passenger service from Cleveland, and Geauga Lake-bound trains stopped fairly close to Luna, at East 93rd Street, to board parkgoers.

Although not an amusement park, the Cleveland Industrial Exposition attracted 650,000 people and effectively drew attendance away from all of the Cleveland area parks. Situated on the West Wing Plaza of Public Hall, the Exposition ran for twenty-three days during August of 1927. The central feature was the Tower of Jewels, which was illuminated by thirty-six large searchlights and concealed the most powerful loud speaker in the world. The Exposition also offered visitors fireworks, strolling entertainers, acres of exhibits, Oscar Babcock's loop the loop act, and its biggest draw, an aging John Philip Sousa and his band. Sousa, more than anything else, accounted for the large crowds. It is impossible to review the decline of Luna Park during the late 1920s without pointing to the Cleveland Industrial Exposition as a contributing factor in the park's demise. The slight recession that accompanied the Exposition in 1927 also helped make the season less than ideal.

Throughout its history, Luna had never been without serious competition. However, as a new and financially solid park in 1905, it was easily able to overshadow White City and Euclid Beach. As Euclid Beach developed and became a strong competitor, as new parks opened their gates, and as the automobile made trips to distant parks more feasible, Luna was less able to withstand the competition. Even more detrimental to Luna, and in fact to all amusement parks, was the lethal combination of radio, the movies, and family motor vacations.

The 1920s witnessed the birth of the mass urban mind: a restless new spirit with adequate income, a good deal of leisure time, and an insa-tiable appetite for entertainment. The embryonic movie industry met the demand head-on. Between 1922 and 1929, an average of forty million movie tickets were sold each week. In Cleveland, about seventy movie houses flourished during the early 1920s, and several new movie palaces were constructed. The leg-revealing chorus lines at Luna Park could hardly be expected to compete with the Rialto, when that theater exhibited such suggestive films as *The Love Expert, Sex, Partners of the Night,* and *Romance.* Even when the movie titles did not suggest sex, long lines of ticket holders waited to see their favorite Western heroes or Rin Tin Tin. Unlike the area's vaudeville theaters, which usually closed during the hot summer months of Luna's season, the movie houses operated almost every day of the year. Many even boasted of air conditioning systems that made their seats a great deal more pleasant than an amusement park's steaming pavement.

Even more accessible entertainment was offered by radio. Station KDKA went on the air in Pittsburgh on November 2, 1920, and by the winter of 1921-22, radio had proved to be more than a temporary fad. Cleveland's first station, WHK, began broadcasting in 1922, WJAX soon followed, as did WTAM in 1923. Cleveland newspapers began publishing daily schedules of radio programming and devoting pages, and sometimes sections, to the new industry. In 1922 Americans spent $60,000,000 on radio equipment. By 1929 these annual expenditures reached almost $843,000,000.

Parks tried to come to terms with the radio industry by broadcasting live from dance halls, by convincing radio stations to sponsor park events, and finally, by turning to radio advertising to augment newspaper campaigns. Except for advertising, however, these efforts were in vain. The cruel fact was that people who gathered around a radio set on the front porch on a warm summer night were not visiting amusement parks. The amusement park manager was totally unarmed in his battle with a radio industry that emerged at whirlwind speed.

It is impossible to overstate the influence of the automobile on the evolution of the amusement park and the summer resort. When Luna opened in 1905, only one in every eleven hundred Americans owned an automobile and few people ventured more than five miles from their homes for picnics or other diversions. Those who could afford to visit seaside or mountain resorts traveled by train and stayed for several weeks. With the automobile, however, one day trips of 100 miles and week-long vacations on the highway became common. In 1924, automobile dealers sold 500,000, vehicles and four years later there were 24,000,000 automobiles on the streets. Twenty years after Luna Park opened, the nation boasted one car for every five Americans. The impact of the automobile was different at each park and summer resort. Cedar Point probably benefited more than most from the motoring craze. Originally, everyone who came to Cedar Point arrived by steamship, but the park's president, George Boeckling, recognized the role the automobile would play in the resort industry and constructed a road to the Point in 1914. By 1924, sixty percent of Cedar Point's visitors arrived in automobiles. Of course, Cedar Point was several hours from most cities and proved an ideal destination for one day

By the 1920s, many of Luna's patrons arrived by automobile.
Cleveland *Plain Dealer*

trips. On the other hand, Luna Park was seriously injured by the automobile. After 1920, fewer people arrived at the park on streetcars. Gradually, management expanded parking facilities to handle fifty-five hundred cars, and parking with extra security was provided in the old motordrome. Certainly, there were many days when Luna's parking lots overflowed, but in general, the ability of families to drive to Chippewa Lake, Geauga Lake, Buckeye Lake, and Indian Lake caused a decline in Luna's attendance.

The movies, radio, and the automobile undermined the amusement park industry throughout the 1920s. After wrestling with these competitors, the glassy-eyed park managers were probably unshaken by the news that the amusement park's traditional dress code would be shattered when women started wearing trousers by 1925! Dress codes were now the least of his concerns.

In addition to newspapers, Luna continued to advertise on streetcars throughout the 1920s. Cleveland *Press* Collection, Cleveland State University

Even though steetcar patronage declined during the 1920s, thousands still arrived at Luna by rail.
Bruce Young Collection

Compared to when the park opened in 1905, Luna's midway had a cluttered look during the 1920s.
Author's Collection

RIDES REROUTED

The management of Luna Park fought against decreased attendance and increased competition by adding rides and attractions, initiating promotions, and making a greater effort to solicit group picnics. In general, Luna's management, or more accurately the park's concessionaires, did a good job of replacing older rides and installing some of the industry's newest thrillers. By 1921, all that was left of pre-1910 Luna were the Shoot-the-Chutes, the Old Mill, and the Scenic Railway. Gone were the Rainbow Dips, the Figure Eight coaster, the Circle Swing, and several of the older funhouses. After a new Dodgem ride was installed in 1922, the park's midway lineup included:

New for the 1922 season was the Dodgem. Seen here is its entrance, located behind the High Striker. It is uncertain whether the young gentleman is about to ride or strike.
Richard F. Hershey Collection

Jack Rabbit Coaster	Dodgem
Carousel	Scenic Railway
Airplane Swing	Ferris Wheel
Shoot-the-Chutes	Bug House
Uncle Bim's House	The Luna Arcade
Old Mill	Gyroplane
The Whip	

The Jack Rabbit was Luna's most popular roller coaster.
Cleveland *Plain Dealer*

Early models of the Dodgem had steering mechanisms that took the car in an opposite direction from the turn of the wheel. The Luna ride may have had such vehicles.

Richard F. Hershey Collection

Manager William Reutener once noted that, "The average Clevelander wants something daring. He wants speed. This is why the Chutes, the Jack Rabbit and the other swiftly moving rides are so popular." Privately, the management of Luna might have conceded that both the Chutes and the Jack Rabbit were a bit slow and unequal to the modern, fast rides being built during the 1920s. During that decade, the Big Dipper coaster appeared at Gordon Gardens, the Thriller at Euclid Beach, the Cyclone at Puritas Springs, the Pippin at Summit Beach, and the Cyclone at Cedar Point. All were excellent, contemporary designs by the best amusement engineers of the age and at least one, the Cedar Point Cyclone, was among the most bone-jarring coasters in the region. The roller coaster-building boom of the 1920s made the absence of a large, high-speed coaster at Luna quite obvious.

As the city of Cleveland expanded its recreational facilities, beaches like the one at Edgewater Park gave Luna's pool a great deal of competition.
Cleveland Public Library

WINDS OF CHANGE

When the 1927 season opened, park visitors were greeted by major changes in Luna's appearance and attractions. The once-popular swimming pool was abruptly closed at the start of the 1927 season and never reopened. Obviously, competition from Cleveland municipal pools and beaches finally washed away the novelty of Luna's pool. In fact, by the 1920s municipal bathing beaches in 218 American cities claimed an annual attendance of 40,000,000. Every amusement park with bathing facilities faced competition from municipally operated pools and beaches. In addition, it was becoming increasingly difficult to exclude people from swimming facilities for racial reasons. When Luna opened, there were less than ten thousand African-Americans in Cleveland. By the 1920s, the number was approaching seventy thousand. While it had once been possible to blatantly forbid blacks from entering Luna's swimming facility, it was now easier to close the facility than to face pressure for admittance.

(right) Not far from Luna Park was the excellent city-owned pool at Woodland Hills Park.
Cleveland Public Library

(inset-top) The winner of a bathing beauty contest at Luna's swimming pool during the mid-1920s.
Author's Collection

(inset-bottom) A swimmer at Lake Luna attired in the popular bathing fashions of the 1920s.
Gertrude Lint Collection

Make no bones about it, the great mastodon proved to be
an unpopular exhibit on Luna's midway.
The Cleveland Museum of Natural History

purchase the giant fossil only if the museum would agree to allow him to exhibit the mastodon at Luna Park for two seasons. The museum agreed and Bramley indicated that the park would cover all costs of installation, building construction, insurance, and the return of the exhibit to the museum after the 1928 season.

The bones were prepared and assembled at New York's American Museum of Natural History, and in March of 1927, nine huge crates arrived at the new exhibit building at Luna. The park gave its new star a good deal of publicity; even going so far as to distribute handbills throughout Cleveland. However, the public showed little interest and few people paid the admission charge to see the impressive masto-

don. By July, park manager Bluem reported that admissions were not even paying the salaries of the guards and the ticket takers. He asked if the museum would agree to pay the $283 insurance premium, and having no alternative, the museum's board agreed. Attendance did not improve, and in February of 1928, Bluem begged the museum to accept the mastodon for their collection immediately rather than waiting for the end of the next season. He also asked the museum to pay for moving the weighty exhibit. Again the museum agreed, and park management was much relieved to have Bramley's pet project removed from the midway.

Fred Bramley, with Mrs. Bramley, at the time of one of his archeological expeditions.
Cleveland Public Library

MAKING SPORT AT LUNA

Clearly, the public did not share his interest in natural history. The whole affair also suggested that people visited amusement parks to be entertained, not to be educated. To paraphrase one eminent historian of the 1920s, if investing in business ventures was considered great sport, then at the same time, sports had become a great business. Although professional football was only marginally popular, collegiate football emerged as a national pastime and lucrative business. Knute Rockne, Red Grange, the Four Horsemen, and Centre College were big news on the sports pages and at the admission turnstiles. The 1920s witnessed the construction of huge new college stadiums at schools like Ohio State, Michigan, Yale, Illinois, and California. By 1927, thirty million spectators were paying $50 million a year to watch college football.

Except for League Park, which was used mostly for baseball, Cleveland lacked a major stadium for collegiate games, professional football, and other events. Recognizing this, Harold Gould, the assistant sales manager of the Fairchild Milling Company, organized a group of investors and formed the Luna Park Athletic Field Company during the spring of 1926. The company entered into an agreement with the Luna Park Amusement Company and secured a concession to build and operate a stadium just outside of the park's walls. The new stadium was designed and built by the M. E. Nelson Company of Cleveland and cost about forty thousand dollars to construct. Luna Stadium was rectangular and its fifty-foot wide bleachers seated forty thousand. With added seating at ground level, the stadium's capacity could be expanded to seventy-six thousand. One of the main purposes for constructing the stadium was to provide a home for Cleveland's new professional football team, the Panthers. General Zimerman obtained the American Football League franchise for the team and also served as vice president of the nine-team league. The team opened its home schedule on September 26, 1926, before 22,000 spectators. Clad in gold and black, the Panthers faced the New York Yankees. Led by Illinois gridiron hero Red Grange, the Yankees boasted powerful backfield recruits from Alabama, Iowa, Colgate, and Columbia. As one reporter predicted, the Panthers ". . . face what looks like an impossible task to stop Grange and his famous running mates. . . ." Although Grange enjoyed a twenty-one yard gallop, the Panthers won by a score of 10-0. The Panthers won two of their next three games, but attendance fell to only about a thousand spectators per game. In November the team was sued by an advertising company for non-payment of debts and the franchise went into receivership. Following this, the league disenfranchised the team and it was disbanded. Interestingly, the Panther name was originally selected for the team that would become the Cleveland Browns many years later.

Following the disbanding of the Panthers, many of the players were recruited by the Cleveland Bulldogs, which played their 1927 season at Luna Stadium. Originally the legendary Canton Bulldogs, the financially embarrassed team was bought by Samuel H. Deutsch and brought to Cleveland in 1924. The Bulldogs played their 1924-25 games at Dunn Field before being sold to a new owner in 1926. In 1927, Deutsch and a group of investors including Harold Gould, again bought the team and brought them to Gould's stadium. The team signed Michigan quarterback Benny Friedman and opened the home season against the New York Giants. However, the team finished fourth in the league with a mediocre 8-4-1 record. After the season, the Bulldogs were sold to a Detroit owner who moved them to Michigan and renamed them the Detroit Wolverines.

Although professional football was never again played at Luna Stadium, the facility had a distinguished career as home for the John Carroll University football team. For a number of years the John Carroll squad was coached by Mal Elward, a former teammate of Knute Rockne at Notre Dame. Elward's 1924 team, playing before the stadium was built, rolled up 260 points to the opposition's 60.

Football, however, was not the only sport presented at the new Luna Stadium. Both Federal League baseball and Triple A sandlot were tried for awhile. In one of the featured doubleheaders of 1927, the Public Services Tires battled the Tellings, and the Gold Bond Brews faced the Lyon Tailors. Soccer was also popular during the 1920s, especially with Cleveland's ethnic groups. On weekends, teams of Scots, English, Germans, Hungarians, and other nationalities met to play each other and out-of-town teams at Luna Park or Woodland Hills Park. A major event of 1927 was the arrival of the Maccabees soccer team from Palestine. The team was on a summer tour of the United States to play local teams and "...to raise the Jewish people to a level in athletics comparable with that attained by other races." The Maccabees faced a Cleveland team comprised of players from six local soccer teams.

In addition to sporting events, Luna Stadium was perfect for a variety of other outdoor spectator activities. For instance, in June of 1927, the Greater Cleveland Council of the Boy Scouts of America sponsored a huge rally of six thousand scouts in the stadium. That same season, the Veterans of Foreign Wars brought the King Brothers' Wild West Rodeo to the stadium for two weeks. Directed by Colonel Jack King, the show featured two hundred cowboys, cowgirls, Indians, and clowns, as well as three hundred horses, wild bulls, and cattle. The headliner of the show was Midnight, the "greatest jumping horse."

Unfortunately, sprawling Luna Stadium was almost destroyed before the end of its second season. During a firework display on the night of August 10, 1927, an aerial bomb landed unnoticed on the stadium's wooden seats. Later that night, the smoldering fire erupted alerting watchman William Angelo who sounded the alarm. Before the fire could be brought under control, the west and north sides of the stadium had been destroyed, the fence around the park was blazing, and telephone poles on Woodhill Avenue smoked and glowed. Damage was extensive, but Gould and his company spent seventy-four thousand dollars to rebuild and improve the stadium in time for the John Carroll football season.

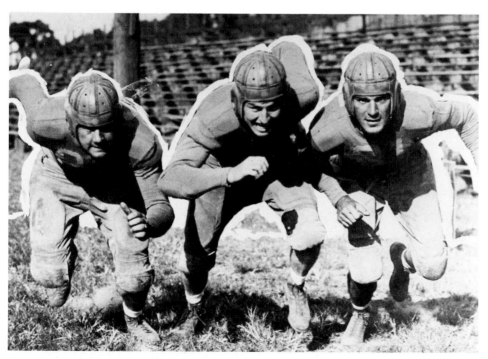

Part of the John Carroll squad at Luna Stadium.
John Carroll University Archives

After the park season ended, the John Carroll University football games brought large crowds at Luna Stadium.
John Carroll University Archives

ZIMERMAN'S DEATH LEADS TO LUNA'S DEMISE

Luna suffered a tragic blow in November of 1926, when General Charles X. Zimerman died in New York City of peritonitis. His body was returned to Cleveland where he lay in state at the Cleveland Grays Armory. He was buried with full military honors at Lake View Cemetery. General Zimerman had been Luna's most respected and capable manager, and one who enjoyed particularly cordial relationships with both the media and the politicians. His death came at a time when Luna could ill afford to lose Zimerman's leadership capabilities.

As a replacement for Zimerman, Fred Bramley selected another respected national guard officer, Clarence F. Bluem. Born in Cleveland in 1888, Bluem was well educated. He earned a master's degree from the University of Wisconsin and was a medical student at Western Reserve University before being hired as a chemist for the East Ohio Gas Company. Fluent in both German and French, Bluem travelled the world extensively in 1909-10. His national guard career began in 1914 when he enlisted as a private in Battery A, First Ohio Volunteer Artillery. He served at the Mexican border, and went to France as a captain in the 134th Field Artillery. After the war, he commanded the 135th Field Artillery and took some time off from his duties as Luna's manager to study at the army's artillery school at Fort Sill. At Luna, Colonel Bluem surrounded himself with a team that included Nick Sutmaier, assistant manager; R. C. Walsh, advertising and publicity manager; J. W. Pendlebury, assistant to Walsh; and F. C. "Red" Watson, general announcer.

Like Zimerman, Bluem took immediate command of Luna Park. In 1927, he temporarily suspended all advertising and left on a tour of east coast parks and resorts. He was very impressed by the fact that many parks were expanding their kiddieland sections. Upon his return to Luna, Bluem purchased live ponies for children to ride and plans were made for the construction of a fully-equipped kiddieland at the park. Aware that stage shows were losing money, he quickly abandoned both vaudeville and musical shows and decided to convert the outdoor theater into a summer movie house. Bluem then signed an agreement with Rayart

Pictures Corporation to bring "first-run" movies to the park. Movies that had never been screened in Cleveland were shown on Monday and Tuesday nights, while other movies were presented during the remainder of the week. Had the Luna Park Amusement Company's fortunes not been on the decline, Colonel Bluem might have done great things with the park. As it was, he spent the next three seasons simply trying to meet payroll expenses and juggle bills.

As all of these changes were taking place, Fred Bramley was noticeably absent from the park. His venture in the automobile industry, negotiations to buy a mastodon, and several archeological expeditions kept him quite busy. However, he was not exactly out of the spotlight. On August 22, 1928, he was entertaining friends on his yacht when the boat was hailed by a Coast Guard cutter searching for rum runners. When Bramley failed to respond, the cutter fired a shot and then rammed Bramley's boat. Still resisting boarders, Bramley demanded that the cutter follow him to Rocky River. There was no liquor on Bramley's boat, but the stubborn yachtsman turned the whole episode into a major publicity event. Coast Guard officers insisted that pleasure craft were becoming major carriers of illegal liquor, while Bramley loudly proclaimed that his rights had been unfairly violated. In retrospect, his time would have been better spent in getting publicity for Luna as the park headed toward its final season.

Fred Bramley at the helm of his boat. In a much pubicized incident, Bramley refused to submit to a Coast Guard for contraband liquor.
Cleveland *Plain Dealer*

HAPTER SIX

Weeds and tall grass grow in front of Luna's deserted entrance during the summer of 1930.
Cleveland *Plain Dealer*

THE DEMISE OF LUNA PARK

THE GOLDEN ERA BEGINS TO TARNISH

The 1920s, despite a recession at the beginning of the decade and the threat of financial disaster throughout the period, are generally thought of as a decade of prosperity. Most amusement parks and summer resorts made money, at least during the middle years of the decade. However, few park owners realized that the Gilded Age of the amusement park ended at about the same time that the World War armistice took effect. The Great Depression that came after 1929 only served to hasten a decline in the amusement park business that was already well underway.

The reasons for the decline of the amusement park, as it existed about 1910, are many: an over-saturation of the market with too many parks; the loss of revenues from alcoholic beverages during Prohibition; a new family mobility brought about by widespread ownership of automobiles; the rise of commercial radio as a form of family entertainment; the increasing popularity of motion pictures; and the fact that the amusement park was no longer the novelty that it had been. Each of these factors either reduced park profits or siphoned customers away to enjoy other entertainments.

Inexorably, national trends and government regulations chipped away at the very foundation of the amusement park. Prohibition had the most immediate and devastating effect, although not every park operated bars. Euclid Beach, which stopped serving alcoholic beverages in 1901, was essentially unaffected by the dry era. Euclid Beach was, however, an anomaly. Most parks and summer resorts derived much of their income from beer, liquor, and wine. Some, like Luna Park, served only beer. Others, notably Cedar Point, dedicated entire buildings to full bar service. Obviously, prohibition devastated the big resorts such as Coney Island, Atlantic City, and Cedar Point. A major source of income was gone, and only the urban prosperity of the mid-1920s partially offset the loss of revenue. Many of Luna's customers were first and second generation Germans, Bohemians, Hungarians, and Irish. For them, beer was a tradition, and the availability of it was a major reason that they favored Luna Park over Euclid Beach. When the German Village could no longer serve beer, Luna lost some of its popular appeal.

In addition to national trends, local factors made life difficult for the management of Luna Park. When the park first opened in 1905, Luna's great advantage over Euclid Beach was its proximity to comfortable working-class neighborhoods. This, combined with efficient streetcar service helped make Luna an instant success and kept it a viable business venture until the end of the World War.

The migration of the working class to suburbia proceeded slowly before the war. But by the 1920s the exodus from city to suburb was very pronounced. The percentage of residents in Cuyahoga County who lived within Cleveland's city limits declined from eighty-eight percent in 1910 to seventy-five percent in 1930. Even the solid ethnic communities were beginning to disperse to the east, southeast, and west. As the people moved out of the city the core of Cleveland began a long period of decay. This population shift had an unfortunate effect on Luna Park. Those who could best afford to spend money in the park were moving further away and to areas not served by the Cleveland streetcar system. The street railway system had been Luna's best ally, but streetcar patronage peaked in 1920 and then began a sharp decline that lasted until the Depression.

As the population moved out of the city's core, the new suburban populations began to favor other parks over Luna. Those who moved east or southeast were now much closer to Euclid

A new Templar automobile parked in front of Fred Bramley lakeside home for a publicity photo.
Western Reserve Historical Society

BRAMLEY'S DISTRACTIONS UNDERMINE LUNA'S ATTRACTIONS

Beach and Geauga Lake Park. To the west, Puritas Springs Park, Crystal Beach Park in Vermilion, and even Cedar Point were now within easy driving distance. And, those people who moved south of Cleveland were just a short drive from Chippewa Lake Park in Medina County.

At a time when the American amusement park was past its zenith and Luna required both constant attention and increased investments, Fred Bramley seemingly lost interest in the park. Bramley had never lacked for activity, and his paving company, the source of his wealth, was always his first concern. The fact that he relinquished day-to-day management of Luna to Zimerman suggests that Luna was never his major business priority.

By the time of the World War, Bramley was committed to many new adventures; Luna Park had become more of a burden than an enjoyment. In 1916, Bramley organized the Templar Motors Corporation and began producing a quality automobile that was the equivalent of the modern sports car. During the war, he switched production to artillery shells and employed more than a thousand workers. After the war, automobile production resumed, but the post-war recession and the narrow market for the Templar forced the company into receivership. Despite building six thousand cars, the company stopped production in 1924. Bramley and a large number of other investors lost more than six million dollars.

A few years later, all of Bramley's attention turned to a project inspired by a dream he had in 1928. In his dream, Bramley saw a submerged island located somewhere off the Pacific Coast. Incredibly, he travelled to California and hired an airplane to search for the island of his dreams. Even more incredibly, he found an island about 100 miles from San Pedro, California. Unfortunately, it was also about fifteen feet below the ocean's surface. Undaunted, Bramley planned to raise the island and become the ruler of the new land mass. He spent several months planning how to construct a breakwall around the island, and pump the water out of the enclosed area, thus creating a new island. Finally, in 1930, he suspended further plans and announced that the raising of the island was financially impractical.

While neither the Templar Motors failure nor the dream island diversions were directly related to Luna Park, Bramley's attentions were directed away from the park almost continually from 1916 until the late 1920s. The executive and financial leadership that he contributed from 1911 through the landmark season of 1915 were lacking at a time when the company most needed Bramley's abilities. Only the managerial skills and devotion of General Zimerman kept Luna going. But even this was not enough, for by 1926 the park company was only marginally profitable.

INTEREST IN LUNA DRIES UP

Once the darling of Cleveland area amusement parks, Prohibition and the growth of suburbia were working against Luna Park. For two decades, Luna had outshined and outlived parks like White City and Willoughbeach Park. Luna was Cleveland's favorite amusement park, and as pleasant as Euclid Beach was before the World War, it usually played second fiddle to Luna. Luna Park was considered a model operation, and when Akron's Summit Beach Park was built in 1917 it was Luna that served as the design inspiration.

Luna Park's dominance began to fade with Prohibition in 1919. With beer sales gone and old entertainment forms like concert bands losing ground to jazz, the edge that Luna once held over Euclid Beach dissipated. At the same time, the Humphrey family earmarked large budgets for the installation of rides like the Great American Racing Derby, the Thriller coaster, the Mill Chute, and the largest Dodgem building in the United States. By 1925, Euclid Beach had won the contest for Cleveland's entertainment dollar.

When the 1929 season opened, however, the fact that Luna was about to collapse was not evident. Even Bramley, off on his search for an island, never dreamed that by August his park would be beyond salvation. Had he listened to much of the bad news emanating from parks around the country, he might have realized what was happening. By 1927, Luna's short-lived competitor, Gordon Gardens, was acquired by the city for $365,000 and was slated to become part of Gordon Park. Amusements were discontinued in August of 1927, and during the next few years much of the park was destroyed by fires of suspicious origin. In western Pennsylvania, the owners of Conneaut Lake Park were declared bankrupt and their company handed to a receiver. Their $554,000 in liabilities were offset by only $10,000 in accessible assets. At Cedar Point, President George Boeckling predicted a dark economic future and curtailed all expansion plans.

Oblivious to the ominous signs, Luna blissfully opened on May 15. Indeed, Bramley authorized Bluem to spend a great deal of money on the park during the winter of 1928-29. Many of the buildings were repainted, and strings of colored lights were suspended above the midway. Kiddyland received a facelift and the Old Mill was converted into the Mystic Cavern. Two hundred and fifty recently-purchased monkeys inhabited Monkey Island. Concessionaire Harold Gould polished and painted Luna Stadium. Opening day was crowded, and Colonel Bluem declared it the best season opener since 1917. The only indication that anything was different from previous years was the very light advertising schedule that the park placed in local newspapers. Traditional early-season advertising was almost non-existent and even free publicity seems to have been in short supply.

A souvenir from Luna's final season.   James Abbate Collection

Outwardly, everything seemed normal at Luna; events took place just as they had for the past twenty-five seasons. Free movies were shown every afternoon and evening. On the Fourth of July the traditional firework display exploded over the park. In the ballroom, the house band (Horace Vokoun and his Luna Park Lunatics) continued to flood the dance floor with melody. Often, Vokoun's dance sets were broadcast from the dance hall over WHK Radio. At Luna Stadium there were the usual weekend soccer matches, and in July, eleven amateur boxing bouts were promoted. Picnic groups remained loyal to their favorite park. Two of the groups that used the park almost from the day it opened, the Al Sirat Grotto and the Republican Party, scheduled events as usual. The Republican picnic, held on August 31, was the last major event ever held at Luna. As normal as everything appeared, Bramley returned from a trip in July to find that gate receipts had declined by thirty-six percent. The sad fact was that there was not enough money coming into the park to meet the weekly payroll and to service all of the company's debts.

As the park limped through a difficult season, fate continued to work against Luna. On the night of August 8, Lieutenant Philip Saginor of the park police department discovered an out-of-control fire consuming Luna Stadium. More than thirty thousand spectators watched as nine fire companies and more than one hundred firemen fought the blaze. Standing in a deepening lake caused by their fire hoses, the firefighters battled to halt the spread of flames and to save the nearby roller coaster. The heat

from the huge conflagration was intense. The park's high board fence smoldered and caught fire, as did telephone poles along Woodhill Road. Trolley lines fell with a shower of sparks and stores on Woodhill lost electric power. When it was over, most of the stadium's walls had collapsed and concessionaire H. C. Gould's losses reached sixty thousand dollars. Despite the fact that only thirty thousand dollars of the damage was covered by insurance, Gould assured President B. J. Rodman of John Carroll University that the stadium would be rebuilt in time for the school's football opener on September 28. Gould kept his promise and the John Carroll squad, apparently pleased with the reconstructed stadium, crushed Valparaiso, 90-0.

The temporary loss of the stadium meant an immediate decline in park attendance. The All Nations Festival, scheduled for three days after the fire, was nearly cancelled. Its soccer games, anticipated as big moneymakers, had to be cancelled, but the remainder of the event went on as planned. The Festival featured numerous ethnic performances, including Polish and Ukrainian dancers, a Chinese opera, a Hindu play, German signing societies, Norwegian folk dancers, a Syrian sword fight, and a glimpse at a typical Croatian home. Despite the curtailing of activities caused by the loss of the stadium, the festival was declared a success.

At about the time of the fire, Luna's financial situation suddenly collapsed. The Pippin Coaster Company, operator of the Pippin coaster, the June Bug, and the Caterpillar, initiated legal action against the Luna Park Amusement Company. In its struggle to make payments to debtors, the park had failed to provide the Pippin Coaster Company with the concessionaire's share of the ticket revenues from its attractions. The park's inability to pay the Pippin Coaster Company was particularly embarrassing. The concession company was formed in 1922 and within three years operated a trio of major rides at Luna. The park company collected the daily receipts for the rides, returning fifty percent of the Pippin coaster's ticket sales and sixty-five percent of the income from the June Bug and the Caterpillar. All went smoothly until July of 1927 when Luna stopped making the weekly payments. In fact, by the end of 1928, the park owed the Pippin Coaster Company $13,500. Robert B. Loehr, one of the primary owners of the concessions, negotiated with park management and agreed to a settlement. The park would pay the Pippin Coaster Company $10,500, retaining $2,500 in return for painting the Pippin coaster for the 1930 season. However, the park company's ability to pay did not improve, and by August of 1929, the Pippin Coaster Company was owed fourteen thousand dollars. As a result, the Luna Park Amusement Company and one of its best concessionaires became bitter enemies.

Late in August, the Whistle Bottling Company, supplier of soft drinks to the park, petitioned the courts to appoint a receiver for the park company. The park owed the bottler $885.75, and when a partial payment was made, the bank returned the check for insufficient funds. Correctly assuming that the park company was insolvent, the bottler felt that a receiver was its only hope.

Troubles mounted for Luna Park. It failed to make payments on a sixty thousand dollar loan originally due in July of 1928. The Guardian Savings & Trust Company filed suit, and an attorney, Herman J. Nord, was appointed by the court as receiver for the Luna Park Amusement Company. Soon after, the Stearn Advertising Company obtained a judgement against the park company for $4,378, and the court ordered that chairs, tables, pianos, cash registers, the skating rink, the North Wind roller coaster, and various other rides be offered at a sheriff's sale to satisfy the debt. Nord asked for an injunction halting the sale and successfully argued that the park should not be offered piecemeal but should be sold as a whole.

The summer of 1930. The foundation of the June Bug is visible in the background and wires hang from disconnected lamps. On the left is the abandonded station of the Pippin coaster.
Cleveland *Plain Dealer*

THE LAST OF LUNA PARK. Wreckers yesterday began razing the old dance hall at Luna Park, once considered the most beautiful amusement park in Ohio. The land has been sold to an allotment company.

Erasing Luna, June 23, 1931. Richard F. Hershey Collection

AFTER TWENTY-FIVE SEASONS, LUNA PASSES TO A MEMORY

During the winter of 1929-30, the park stood silent and its future remained uncertain. Colonel Bluem, equally uncertain of his own future, agreed to serve as statutory agent for the company, and all tax notices and claims were sent to his attention. Finally, on May 2, 1930, a sheriff's sale was held to satisfy the eleven major creditors of the Luna Park Amusement Company. According to a presale estimate, the park was valued at $215,000. However, with the nation's economy crumbling, there were few investors interested in an insolvent amusement park. As a result, J. Harold Bramley, son of the park's president, purchased the park at the bargain price of $72,534. In addition, he agreed to assume the $106,200 mortgage.

With the park still in the possession of the Bramley family, and still actually controlled by Fred Bramley, there was speculation that Luna would open on schedule in May. However, the younger Bramley promptly announced that Luna was in need of major repairs. Improvements, he stated, might take all summer. In the meantime, if someone wanted to lease the park immediately, it could open in 1930. If not, Bramley planned to reopen the gates in 1931.

The drained lagoon of the Shoot-the-Chutes and the remains of Monkey Island. Around the lagoon, little of Luna Park remains.
Cleveland Public Library

Perhaps the Bramleys had never intended to operate the park again, or, if they had, they quickly changed their minds. The economic lessons of a deepening depression were not lost upon the father and son partnership. An amusement park was a poor investment during a depression, and they rapidly came to the conclusion that Luna was finished. On June 23, wreckers began razing the great dance hall. By late July, the Bramleys revealed that within thirty days only the office building and the stadium would be left. As August moved toward September, only the big Ferris Wheel, the ornate carousel, the empty concrete lagoons,and the foundations of buildings remained scattered among piles of colorful wooden debris. The skating rink, however, remained standing and was slated to continue operation.

When demolition started, concessionaires began to sell their equipment or to move it other parks. Arthur Musso still had his food stands at Summit Beach Park and much of his equipment was moved to Akron. Bert Chatfield, Luna's longtime photo studio operator, moved his concession to Chippewa Lake Park. There, he managed a successful studio throughout the 1930s and took many photos that documented life at Chippewa during the Great Depression.

In 1930, Luna's fabulous carousel was sold to Puritas Springs Park. It operated there until Puritas Springs closed in 1958.

Author's Collection

condition, Philadelphia Toboggan #35 may be the only remaining artifact from Luna Park.

Except for the stadium and the roller rink, all of the rides and buildings were gone by the fall of 1930. However, there still remained the problem of what to do with the land. Fred and Harold Bramley announced plans to subdivide the old park, cut streets through the midway, and develop a residential allotment. However, the 1930s were no more agreeable to real estate developers than they were to amusement parks.

In 1932, the Buckeye-Woodhill Council approached Fred Bramley with a proposal to convert part of the park's land to a playground. Bramley not only agreed, but also donated tools and lumber to construct baseball backstops. Shrubs were provided by various groups, a landscape gardener donated his time, and someone loaned horses and implements. However, the project did not get very far, and most of the land remained a junk yard filled with rubbish that had once been a beautiful amusement park. Two years later, a small parcel of Bramley's land was sold to Our Lady of Peace Church. Mass was held in a tent on the site until a church could be constructed.

Luna Stadium, which had been rebuilt after the 1929 fire, stood vacant except for the occasional soccer match or baseball game on weekends. In the spring of 1933, Harry J. Richards and Robert R. Knapp leased the stadium and constructed a cinder and clay motorcycle racing track in the center. The oval track was 150 feet wide and 375 feet long, with a racing surface 25 feet wide. The new track was completed by June 26, but it was not very successful and soon closed.

Since property taxes on the park land were costing the Bramleys twenty-one thousand dollars per year, they kept searching for prospective buyers or ways to develop the property. In 1935, the Ohio Legislature considered legalizing dog racing in Ohio. Ever the showman, Fred Bramley announced plans to establish a dog track in Luna Stadium, but these plans never materialized.

Throughout the worst years of the Depression, the skating rink continued operations. Bramley leased the rink to a local man who kept it open three nights a week. With little or no maintenance, the building became an eyesore and local residents complained about its appearance. In fact, vandals tried seven times to

The foundation of the escalator that once carried park
patrons to the entrance.
Cleveland *Plain Dealer*

The roller skating rink continued to operate until it was
destroyed by fire on December 11, 1938.
Cleveland *Plain Dealer*

With the last of Luna Park cleared, construction began on the Woodhill Homes project.
Case Western Reserve University

torch the building. The seventh time, on December 11, 1938, they were successful. The fire was started by oily rags and paper stuffed under the floor. As biased on-lookers yelled, "Let it burn," barrels of neat's-foot oil used to soften skate leather blazed ferociously. During the eight hour conflagration, eight people were driven from nearby homes by smoke, several houses and a fire truck were damaged, ten firemen were treated for burns, and Fire Captain Roy Haylor died of a heart attack. The building, of no value to Bramley, was uninsured. Nevertheless, fire investigators claimed that the rink fire represented a thirty-five hundred dollar loss. At the time, rumors circulated that one of Luna's unhappy neighbors had started the fire to obliterate the eyesore. If so, he was probably stunned by the resulting injuries, loss of life, and damage.

Financially, the loss of the rink meant little to Bramley for he had already turned his attention to providing Cleveland with some much needed low-cost housing. By the time of the rink fire, the Cleveland Metropolitan Housing Authority already had an option on the land, and with financing from the Federal Housing Authority, moved ahead with plans to build 26 buildings containing 568 dwellings. In June of 1939, four Cleveland companies were awarded contracts totaling $2,344,761, and housing officials in Washington announced that the project would be completed within 12 months. Woodhill Homes, capable of housing 1800 residents, was ready for occupancy in November, 1940. As the years passed, fewer and fewer of the residents knew that they lived on the graveyard of a fascinating amusement park.

By the spring of 1941, every trace of Luna had been obliterated
and replaced with neat, planned housing.
Case Western Reserve University

The neighborhood around Luna, whose character was molded largely by the park, continued to evolve after it closed. In 1932, streetcars entering the area still displayed signs that read "Scovill-Luna Park." Motormen reported that more than one rider, unaware of Luna's demise, stepped off the cars at the park loop only to find the park ruins. On September 26, 1933, service to the old Luna Loop ended and the line's new terminus was established on a wye at Woodland and Quincy Avenues. The Scovill Line itself was terminated on May 7, 1946.

The streets surrounding the park site remained a pleasant Italian neighborhood for many years. To better serve the residents, the Catholic Diocese of Cleveland decided to establish an Italian language church in the area. Our Lady of Mount Carmel (East) was founded by Father William O'Donnell in July of 1936, and a brick basement church was constructed at East 110th and Ingersoll Road. When the land was acquired by the Housing Authority in 1939, a new church was built at Garfield and Ingersoll.

Like all neighborhoods, the area originally dominated by Luna Park also had its darker side. During the Prohibition years, the corner of East 110th and Woodland Avenue became one of the centers of Cleveland's illegal beer and liquor industry. The neighborhood was primarily controlled by the seven Porello brothers, four of whom died in disputes over liquor sales and territories. After James Porello was killed by gun fire on July 27, 1930, the southeast corner of what had been Luna Park became known as the "Bloody Corner."

As memories of Luna Park began to fade, those who had built and operated the park also departed. Bramley remained an active businessman and maintained an interest in Great Lakes boating and in archeology. In 1930, he organized the Bramley-Carter Expedition which investigated the Mayan civilization of Central America. The specter of Luna, however, remained with him until the day he died. At the time the park closed, company bonds were owned by twenty-one individuals and one corporation. Although retiring these bonds would have cost only forty-five hundred dollars, Bramley was either unable or unwilling to make cash payments. On December 24, 1931, he made arrangements for shares of stock in the Cleveland Trinidad Paving Company stock to serve as collateral for these bonds. Finally, in 1939, the trust agent, the Guardian Trust Company, was in the last phase of liquidation and the trust had to be settled. At that time each bondholder received Cleveland Trinidad stock equal to twice the value of their Luna Park bonds. With this action, the last business related to Luna Park was finished.

In February of 1941, Fred Bramley entered Mount Sinai Hospital for major surgery. He never fully recovered and died on May 30, 1941. His son, J. Harold, died in 1957.

One by one, those associated with Luna Park during its last years passed away. Colonel Bluem, the park's last manager, died at Lakeside Hospital following surgery in 1931. He was only forty-two. Possibly the last survivor of Luna's management team was James W. Pendlebury, who was assistant advertising and publicity manager in 1928 and 1929. Pendlebury retired from the United States General Accounting Office in 1962 and died twelve years later in 1974.

With the demise of Luna Park, Cleveland's amusement park scene became a little more sedate, a little less colorful, and a great deal more conservative. Euclid Beach Park, which eclipsed Luna in popularity during the 1920s, became the summertime sweetheart of anyone born in Cleveland after 1930. Somehow, as great as Euclid Beach was, it lacked the racy, chromatic personality of Luna. Winsor French, a popular society columnist and keen judge of his surroundings, blamed Prohibition for Luna's untimely demise. In addition, he thought that perhaps the new generation was just a little too sophisticated for the sensual pleasures of Luna. The fact was that Luna Park, and the entire form of entertainment that was so well received in 1905, had no place in a more modern society.

In an epitaph written two years after Luna closed, French lamented, "Gone too is one of the strongest Continental tangs Cleveland could ever boast of. Luna alone of all our amusement parks achieved the flavor of their original forbears. Only Luna could fire the imagination to picture visions or memories of Paris street fairs, Viennese carnivals and Hungarian gypsies wandering wistfully along the banks of the blond Danube. From its very inception it was a great leveler – where the rich and the poor and the foreign went at the close of hot summer days in search of simple pleasure."

Author's Collection

Richard F. Hershey
Collection

APPENDIX A

**Luna Park – 1910
Cleveland, Ohio**

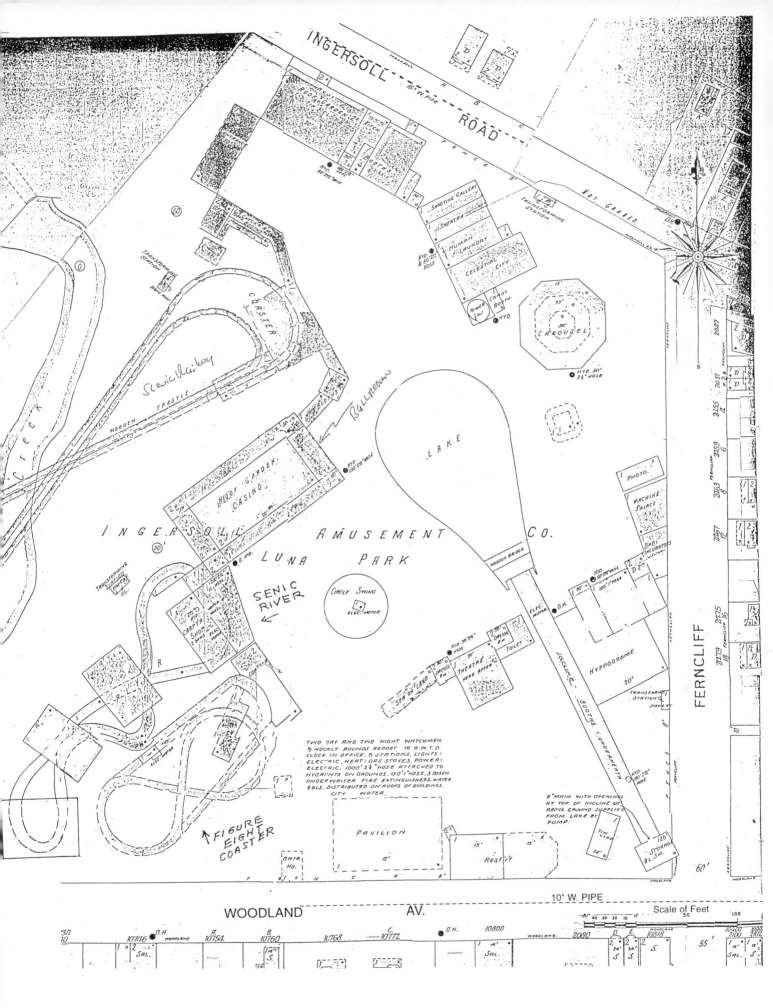

INGERSOLL — — — ROAD

CREEK

SCENIC RAILWAY

WOODEN TRESTLE

COASTER

BALLROOM

I. O. O. F. GARDEN
CASINO

INGERSOLL   AMUSEMENT   CO.

LUNA   PARK

SENIC RIVER

Circle Swing
ELEC. MOTOR

LAKE

WOODEN BRIDGE

SHOOTING GALLERY
THEATRE
HUMAN LAUNDRY
CELESTIAL CITY
TOWER
CANDY BOOTH
HYD.
TRANSFORMING STATION

CAROUSEL

PHOTO.
MACHINE PALACE
BABY INCUBATORS

FERNCLIFF

HYPPODROME
TRANSFORMING STATION

INCLINE
BOOTHS UNDERNEATH

SEA ON LAND
DRESSE RM
THEATRE
HERE AFTER
DRESSE RM
TOILET
ELEC. MOTOR
O.H.

TWO DAY AND TWO NIGHT WATCHMEN.
½ HOURLY ROUNDS REPORT TO A.W.T.D.
CLOCK IN OFFICE, 5 STATIONS. LIGHTS:
ELECTRIC. HEAT: GAS STOVES. POWER:
ELECTRIC. 1000' 2½" HOSE ATTACHED TO
HYDRANTS ON GROUNDS. 150' HOSE, 3 DOZEN
UNDERWRITER FIRE EXTINGUISHERS. WATER
BBLS. DISTRIBUTED ON ROOFS OF BUILDINGS.
CITY   WATER.

6" MAIN WITH OPENINGS
AT TOP OF INCLINE WO
ABOVE GROUND SUPPLIE
FROM LAKE BY
PUMP.

TIN CLAD
STORAGE BL SM.

FIGURE EIGHT COASTER

GATE HO.

PAVILION

REST'T

10" W. PIPE

Scale of Feet

WOODLAND   AV.

APPENDIX B

Luna Park – 1925
Cleveland, Ohio

THE LUNA PARK AMUSEMENT CO.

NIGHT WATCHMAN · EVERY NIGHT IN YEAR · APPROVED
CLOCK - 5 MEN IN PARK ALL NIGHT DURING SEASON.
30 GAL. CHEM. TANK 1600' - 2½" HOSE ATT'D TO HYDS. AS
SHOWN & ON HOSE REEL · CHEMICALS DIST'D · HEAT:
GAS STOVES IN SEVERAL PLACES · LIGHTS & POWER:
ELECTRIC · CITY WATER THRO'OUT ·

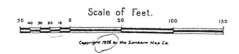

Scale of Feet.

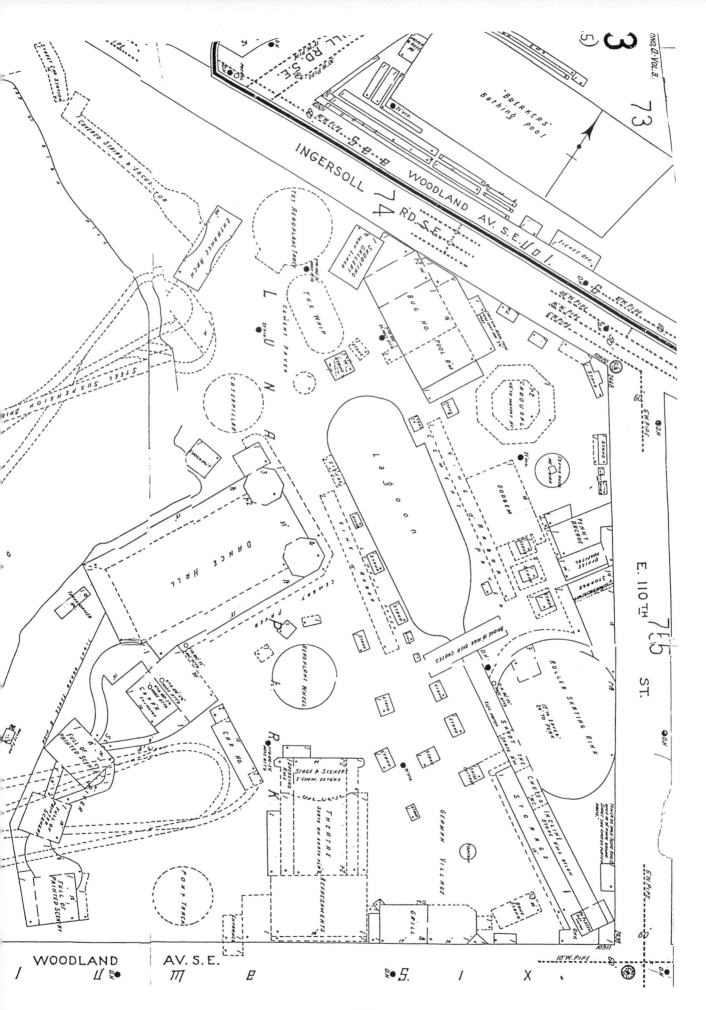

INDEX

LP refers to Luna Park, Cleveland, Ohio

Unless otherwise noted, all rides and attractions are in reference to Luna Park, Cleveland, Ohio.

References to illustrations are in boldface type.

ABOUT THE AUTHORS:

A graduate of Baldwin-Wallace College, David Francis has written more than two dozen magazine and journal articles and has been a contributor to *The Encyclopedia of Southern History.* Diane Francis majored in English at the University of Akron before pursuing a career as an advertising copywriter in Akron and New York.

The Francis' collaboration began in the mid-1980s when they began to research the first edition of *Cedar Point: The Queen of American Watering Places.* Since the publication of their first book, they have co-authored three additional works and are currently working on a fourth.

Building on more than 20 years' experience in the advertising business, the Francis' founded their own advertising company in Wadsworth, Ohio, in 1990. Married since 1981, Dave and Diane share their home with several dogs and cats.